I0483092

WHEN THEY WIN, YOU WIN

WHEN THEY WIN, YOU WIN

A MORE HUMAN APPROACH TO SUPPORTING ENTREPRENEURSHIP

VLAD CAZACU

NEW DEGREE PRESS

COPYRIGHT © 2019 VLAD CAZACU

All rights reserved.

WHEN THEY WIN, YOU WIN

A More Human Approach to Supporting Entrepreneurship

ISBN   978-1-64137-246-6   *Paperback*

          978-1-64137-247-3   *Ebook*

To all the innovators around the world who are working
day and night on building a better future for all of us

CONTENTS

INTRODUCTION

"Unfortunately, folks at Y-Combinator were smarter than us — or, fortunately, I should say, they were smarter than us, and said, 'No, no, it's too early for this. Don't do it.' They rejected us," says Alexis Ohanian, the co-founder of Reddit.

One day following the Y-Combinator rejection, Ohanian described how he got a call from Paul Graham, a co-founder of the accelerator and a legendary investor in Silicon Valley.

"I was like, 'Hello?' and he was like, 'Alexis, we still hate your idea.' 'Really? You called just to say that? We were on our way back to Virginia,'" Ohanian says. But Graham continued on by saying "'No, no, we like you two. Come up with another idea and we will invest. Whatever it is.'"

The next idea the two founders had was Reddit, and Y-Combinator gave them a check for $12,000, 10% of what they usually offered to approved entrepreneurs. Today, over $230 million people visit the site every month making it, as of March 2019, the sixth most visited website in the U.S. and the twenty-first in the world.

SUPPORTING THE ENTREPRENEURS

The world has seen dramatic changes in the way we regard and support company creation. In 1964, we see the first venture capital firm (VC). In the early 1970s, the first startup incubators begin to appear. In 1996, the start-up studio concept comes to life, followed closely by the first startup accelerator in 2005 and the first corporate accelerator in 2006. Soon after, in 2008-2009, the revolution of crowdfunding hit the market and the early 2010s marked the beginning of the venture capital "platform".

The latest research finds that there are around one hundred million new businesses entities created each year all over the world[1]. This has a significant impact on the economies of the world, especially in the job market. The U.S. alone created more than two-and-a-half million new jobs

---

1   Global Report 2017/18. Global Entrepreneurship Monitor. Url: https://www.gemconsortium.org/report.

from entrepreneurial activity in 2015[2]. With these kinds of mind-boggling statistics, it becomes hard to deny the importance of supporting small business founders and their endeavors.

This has clearly not fallen on deaf ears.

Start-up support units such as incubators, accelerators, co-working spaces, innovation hubs, and start-up studios are now found everywhere and their expansion has seen accelerated growth in the past years. With more and more founders choosing to apply and go through these programs every year, it is important to take the time to analyze the actual impact of those units and their evolution throughout time.

It's critical to ask an important question:

What is working?

But perhaps just as important:

What is _not_ working?

---

2   Ibid.

This — it turns out — is the trillion dollar question facing many developed and currently developing business ecosystems around the world.

THREE STORIES OF NEW START-UP ORIGINS

Reddit has become a social powerhouse thanks to its mix of aggregation and user-submitted content, but the website was born out of a different idea altogether.

What started with the initial goal of having a simple way to order food by cell phone from the local Sheetz gas stations turned into one of the world's most visited websites. The two college students founders, Steve Huffman and Alexis Ohanian, were able to grab the attention of Paul Graham, co-founder of the iconic Y-Combinator, after approaching him during a lecture. The plan was ultimately rejected when the duo formally pitched it to the start-up investor in 2005, but Graham promised funding if they could devise something new.

That "something new" turned into Reddit, and three weeks after receiving $12,000 from Y-Combinator and moving to Boston, Ohanian and Huffman pushed out a beta version of the site. The two even started submitting their own links under different usernames to give the illusion of a healthy and functioning site, but Reddit eventually became self-sufficient.

Why did Reddit succeed?

We may never fully understand, but a big part of their success comes from a unique approach that we will be exploring later in the book: investing in people.

Graham decided that the idea was a non-starter, but Ohanian and Huffman had the "it" factor.

Today, it's not uncommon to hear stories of investors "betting on the team" even before the idea has been devised beyond the back of a napkin.

* * *

Yelp, initially an email-based referral service, was started after two former PayPal employees, Jeremy Stoppelman and Russel Simmons, joined the business incubator MRL Ventures in 2004. The original concept failed to attract investors, then Stoppelman caught the flu and had a difficult time finding a recommendation for a local doctor.

"Back then there was very little information on the Internet; it was frustrating," Stoppelman told the *Wall Street Journal* in 2012[3]. "We realized the best way to find a doctor, or other services, was by word of mouth."

After changing the model from email to internet-based, the pair re-launched the concept in 2005. As of 2019, the site averages sixty-nine million unique monthly visitors and continues to expand, predominantly in the mobile app industry.

Even if a personal event shaped the new trajectory of their organization, it would be foolish not to recognize the help they have received from the incubator they were a part of, including the initial one million dollar investment in the young San Francisco-based start-up.

* * *

Airbnb started more or less as a happy accident in 2007 when San Francisco entrepreneurs Joe Gebbia and Brian Chesky were looking to launch "the next big thing." One of the issues with the duo, who met while students at the Rhode Island School of Design, was that they had tons of ideas but not enough money for rent.

3   Loten, Angus. "Search for Doctor Leads to Yelp." *The Wall Street Journal*, Nov. 14, 2012. https://www.wsj.com/articles/SB1000142412 78873245959045781175125897173352.

After finding out that a local design conference had all the city's hotels fully booked, they decided to put three air mattresses on their living-room floor and rent them out in order to raise cash for their living expenses. Six days later, three guests each paid $80 a night. That's when they realized they were onto something, and they never looked back.

"People have said it's the worst idea that ever worked," Chesky said at *Vanity Fair*'s New Establishment Summit in October 2014[4]. "It wasn't supposed to be the big idea; it was supposed to be a way to pay the rent while we thought up the big idea." Airbnb was launched in 2008 and now boasts over six million listings in 191 countries.

During a dinner in November 2008, after incurring thousands of dollars in debt, they received an incredible piece of advice from Michael Seibel, then the CEO of Justin.tv: "Look at you," he said. "You guys are dying. Do Y-Combinator."

After a disappointing interview, and almost missing the cell phone call that announced the decision due to a lack of cell signal on the I-280, the group accepted a $20,000 offer and moved to Mountain View, California. The rest is history.

---

4   Garing, Caleb. "Airbnb Founder: Company "Wasn't Supposed to Be the Big Idea."" *Vanity Fair*, Oct. 2014. https://www.vanityfair.com/news/tech/2014/10/airbnb-founder-big-idea-logo.

WHAT WORKED TODAY PROBABLY
WON'T WORK TOMORROW

With these three start-up triumphs we see that success is derived from accidental innovation, supported through new and novel approaches. Betting on the team and offering an accelerator as a home were all relatively unique approaches at the time in which they were applied to these three start-up successes.

Today? Not so much.

As stated in the Global Accelerator Report in 2016 put together by Gust, 579 accelerator programs around the world have invested over $206 million in 11,305 start-ups[5]. According to the same report, the U.S. and Canada are the most active regions when it comes to investments, while Europe leads in terms of the number of start-ups accelerated[6].

The *Harvard Business Review* found that the number of U.S.-based accelerators increased by an average of 50% every year between 2008 and 2014[7]. With more and more founders all over the world joining these programs, it seems that joining

---

5   Global Accelerator Report 2016. Gust. Url: http://gust.com/
    accelerator_reports/2016/global/.
6   Ibid.
7   Hathaway, Ian. "What Start-up Accelerators Really Do." *Har-vard Business Review*, Mar. 01, 2016. https://hbr.org/2016/03/
    what-start-up-accelerators-really-do.

support units has become the norm for start-ups poised for success. More recently, supporters and investors have experimented with different variations of this model and increased their popularity.

One such variation is the start-up studio, which we will discuss in detail in Chapter 12. Start-up studio guru Attila Szigeti, in his 2015 research, looked at publicly available data for fifty-one studios and two hundred twelve of their portfolio companies and found some exciting trends[8]:

- Funding into portfolio companies has been increasing 48% year-over-year since 2010.

- Since 2008, studio companies have raised more than $4 billion in venture capital.

- Start-up studios create more and more companies, with a 15% increase year-over-year.

- There have been fourteen portfolio companies acquired, and on average, they are acquired three years after their launch.

---

8   Szigeti, Attila. *Start-up Studio Playbook*. 2016.

And that's the rush of innovation -- when something works like it has in these cases, there is a rush to try and duplicate that success.

Case in point: Y-Combinator. While Y-Combinator is certainly the biggest start-up accelerator on the block, with over 1,800 investments and close to 200 exists, there's a question about its recent track record. It is without question that they can point to successful bets on Airbnb, Dropbox, Stripe and Reddit... but since then... their results are less than compelling.

Is that Y-Combinator's fault, or is it due to a new influx of competition, or something else?

Who knows... but we are starting to see that what has worked or is working probably won't work tomorrow.

That's the magic of innovation in many ways — it evolves.

WHAT YOU WILL FIND INSIDE

This book is designed to highlight and explore some of the core elements of entrepreneurial support including:

- Networks, Mentors and Partnerships

- Diversity and Inclusion

- Empathy and Culture

- Entrepreneurial Communities and Ecosystems

- Co-working Spaces

- Incubators & Accelerators

- Start-up Studios

- Universities

- And Much More

While my aim is certainly to look back at what has historically or is currently working, that's probably not why you picked up this book. You want to learn what's next and I trust that through this book, you'll get a clear sense on the future of entrepreneurship support.

Over the past year I set out to talk to and pick the brains of many of the world's leading thinkers, doers, investors, and creators tasked with envisioning the future of entrepreneurial support. I've been fortunate enough to speak with:

- Cyril Ebersweiler, Founder of HAX and General Partner of SOSV

- Hugh Mason, Co-founder and CEO of JFDI.Asia and Adjunct Associate Professor at National University of Singapore

- Jeff Slobotski, Founder of Router Ventures

- Doug Chambers, VP & Global Head of Client Solutions at WeWork

- Matthew Hartman, Partner at Betaworks Ventures

- Ben Elowitz, Managing Director at Madrona Venture Labs

- Rei Wang, Former CEO of Dorm Room Fund

- Jess Williamson, Former EMEA & APAC Director at Techstars

ABOUT THE AUTHOR

I have been in the innovation space for all of my adult life, and a little bit before that if you ask my mom. I have been a founder, twice. The first time, we had to close shop after my business partner left for Japan and the work became too much for a one-person team. The second time, we launched two products, gathered a team of twelve wonderful people, had a fair share of success and are continuing to grow.

I have worked eleven jobs, all before the age of twenty, in industries ranging from food, entertainment, higher education, to strategy consulting and ed-tech. All of this was on a quest to discover what I am passionate about and answer the big question: Who am I? I'm an entrepreneur, an accountant, and a social psychologist who decided to pursue his spark for innovation management.

In the fall of 2017, my team and I approached one of my mentors seeking some guidance on whether we should join a start-up support program or not. It was surprising to have a person, who had been previously incredibly helpful, be very blunt and cold with their advice. I remember them telling us about how we are very young and would not be able to join the start-up full-time and how those programs are for people who can dedicate all of their time to their businesses. That was the moment it struck me that there might be something wrong with this system.

After doing research on the effectiveness of entrepreneurial resources in the educational space, I began to wonder what the larger picture looked like. Armed with a backpack of energy and a full Series A worth of motivation, I began to deeply study and learn more about this subject.

I was lucky enough to have the opportunity to converse with some incredible innovators and conduct over forty research interviews with individuals ranging from the vice president of WeWork, the founder of HAX Accelerator, to the co-founder of JFDI.Asia, and the executives of some of the world's biggest start-up studios such as Betaworks, Pioneer Square Labs, Madrona Venture Labs, and Saturn V.

This journey is narrated from a more journalistic point of view, collecting information from existing research literature in the fields of business, sociology and psychology and intertwining it all with my interviews, my expertise, and my personal experience.

A MORE HUMAN APPROACH

In this book I will follow the argument that entrepreneurial support units are becoming more and more human in their approach, shifting their focus from the start-up itself to the founder and that this will yield higher returns in the long run while showcasing examples from all over the globe. I will also be presenting some of the common indicators of success in this area while arguing that developing a more equitable ecosystem will bring previously underrepresented entrepreneurs to the table and allow them to drive economic development in their areas. I firmly believe that diversity and human relationships are at the core of innovation and only by empowering everyone to create will we be able to witness a design of products based on a true, higher understanding of the market.

I encourage you to join me while I explore the development of entrepreneurial support programs around the world and I can promise that you'll discover:

- How Jeff Slobotski put the Midwest on the map of global entrepreneurship

- How an accelerator experience changed a horseshoe manufacturing and design firm into a social media storytelling start-up

- Why only 2% of venture capital money goes to female founders and how we can change that

- Why culture matters and how not to risk building start-ups where employees have sex and get drunk while at work

- How my passion for design got me to explore co-working spaces on three continents and what I have learned along the way

- How Hugh Mason built the first accelerator in South-East Asia with one thing in mind: community

WHO IS THIS FOR?

This book is written for both founders and managers of entrepreneurial support programs, both stand alone and intra-corporate, as well as for founders interested in joining one such unit and investors interested in backing them. If you fall in none of those categories, don't worry because no matter if you are an angel investor, a business executive, leader, or start-up adviser, you will be able to find a new perspective on the development of the entrepreneurship support ecosystem.

This book is for creative people who believe diversity sits at the core of innovation, who are not afraid to dream big, who are able to bet on humans, not businesses, who build on the ideas of others, and who cannot wait for the product launches to start dreaming about the next one. Throughout my writing, I hope to instill in readers the same sort of passion and excitement that I have for supporting innovation.

At its core, this book is designed to offer a look at the past, present, and future of supporting the next generation of the world's greatest start-ups and new ventures. And like anything that is uncertain, the future that we'll explore is simultaneously exciting and scary. So hop on, fasten your seatbelts, and let's go.

HOW TO USE THIS BOOK

This book is designed to walk you through a series of anecdotes intertwined with recent research and bits of history in order to explain why the new entrepreneurial support equation is: when they win, you win.

THREE PARTS

The first part is the foundation, which sets the stage for the other two by providing a context of the state of innovation management around the world and the current issues companies and start-ups are facing. There is a short conversation about the history of entrepreneurial support, why it was needed in the first place, and where we are now as an industry.

The second part, which is the approach in theory, offers a perspective on the human approach as it relates to many of the activities founders are involved in and the resources they use to accomplish their goals. Each of the five chapters describes a particular angle that is necessary to study in order to understand the bottom line: humans, helped by other humans, design for and sell to humans. It seems that we often forget this .

The third part, the approach in action, offers a glimpse into how specific entrepreneurial support units (also called programs or ESUs throughout the book) are moving towards this new attitude and what you can do to bring your program up to par and succeed. As a founder, this aspect should equip you with the tools necessary to perform your own due diligence before selecting a program to join.

HOW TO READ IT

I would recommend all readers go through the first two sections in order to get an understanding of the Human Approach as a whole. For the third section, the structure is there only to provide options. Treat each chapter in this section as an independent analysis of that particular program type and jump to the ones that interest you most. If you are the manager of a start-up studio it might make sense to start the third part with the twelfth chapter; if you are working at an university-affiliated entrepreneurial center or innovation hub, the thirteenth chapter is your go-to; and so on...

At the beginning of every chapter, there are two or three quotes that should enable you to better grasp the material that follows. I spent a lot of time curating those quotes, so please take a couple of minutes to reflect on them before proceeding to the content.

At the end of every chapter, there are a set of key takeaways summarizing some of the main points discussed. Treat them not as a conclusion but rather as things to consider as you are moving along in the book.

Finally, do not let the structure limit you. Jump to any chapters that grab your attention. Have fun with it all and learn something new.

PART I

THE FOUNDATION

CHAPTER 1

THE CONCEPT OF INNOVATION

"There's no learning without trying lots of ideas and failing lots of times."

— SIR JONATHAN PAUL IVE

"Innovation is the central issue in economic prosperity."

— MICHAEL PORTER

"If you set your goals ridiculously high and it's a failure, you will fail above everyone else's success."

— JAMES CAMERON

The Macintosh in 1984, the computer that brought the graphical user interface to the masses, the iMac in 1998, the stylish desktop computer that popularized the now-ubiquitous USB port, the iPod in 2001, the little device that transformed the record industry by fueling the digital music revolution, the iPhone in 2007, the first real mover in the smartphone arena which started the touch screen revolution, the iPad in 2010, the new way of computing, and the Apple Watch in 2015, the even newer way of computing on our bodies, were all exciting technology advances at the time. All of those and everything in between placed Apple as one of the most innovative companies in the world.

But what exactly was innovative?

In an interview with *The Telegraph* Sir Jonathan Paul Ive, Chief Design Officer at Apple, shared that their "goal is to try to bring a calm and simplicity to what are incredibly complex problems so that you're not aware really of the solution, you're not aware of how hard the problem was that was eventually solved."[9] Innovation in their terms became a quest for elegant problem solving through design.

---

9   Richmond, Shane. "Jonathan Ive Interview: Simplicity Isn't Simple". *The Telegraph*, May 23, 2012. https://www.telegraph.co.uk/technology/apple/9283706/Jonathan-Ive-interview-simplicity-isnt-simple.html.

As an evangelist of design thinking, or human-centered design if you will, I will be treating innovation as a byproduct of good design practices. The Human Approach described is, to some extent, an application on the organization of entrepreneurial support units of those and many more principles.

Why should we care?

For various reasons. First and foremost, because innovation is synonymous with progress. Both are necessary and inexorable — they are part of our human nature, having led us to where we are now and continue to lead us towards the future. We could talk about how the U.S. Census Bureau estimates that young firms (less than six years old) have accounted for 11% of employment and 27% of job creation in 2015 alone[10] and all the other factual benefits of innovation, but I am not trying to convince you that innovation is good.

You many have noticed that in the previous paragraph I put an equal sign between innovation and young firms. Although overly simplified for the moment, I will explore in the coming chapters why start-ups are more likely to be innovative while large corporations will struggle.

---

10   US Census Bureau. Start-up Firms Created Over 2 Million Jobs in 2015. Sep. 20, 2017. Url: https://www.census.gov/newsroom/press-releases/2017/business-dynamics.html.

WE ARE ALL INNOVATORS

Julia Maddox has been an innovator since she was young. Her experience spans many industries from renewable energy, to politics, to higher education, and has landed her into working as the founding director of iZone, the innovation hub at the University of Rochester. When asked how the innovative spark happened, Julia said she was lucky to be born in a family that enthusiastically set her up to be entrepreneurial . Her mother is an art teacher while her dad is a businessman. The convergence of these two mindsets encouraged her to develop a new way of looking at the world — both as an artist and as a ruthless goal setter. She recalls coming up with crazy ideas ever since she was a child.

When Julia was seven years old, she had an operation on her foot. Where other people would see an impediment, she saw a business opportunity. There is this magical vibe of two metal rods with padding when they are brought at school, "Crutches are cool when you are seven" she says. With everyone fighting to try her crutches, Julia started asking for twenty-five cents for a trip back and forth across the playground. Again, we are talking about a 7-year-old who was making money by renting her crutches to other kids. At the time she didn't think of herself as an entrepreneur, but twenty years later she was becoming one. Was the job creative or innovative? It might be a stretch to say yes, but nonetheless we could see the way her family influenced on how Julia saw the world and later prompted her to start her own business and help create others.

Problems are waiting to be solved and profit is always on the table for the trained eye. The issue is that when we are kids, these things seem natural to us and we are not afraid to question things, come up with radical ideas, and be fearlessly creative. In Julia's words, "our pragmatic society beats it out of us during adolescence."

So where does this stem from?

In Julia's case, innovation came from a point of pain. In a conversation with Noel Joyce, head of design at HAX which is the largest hardware accelerator in the world, this topic came up and he slightly disagreed. Prior to his time at SOSV and HAX Noel served with the Irish military for five years, during which he completed a tour of duty in Liberia, West Africa. A mountain biking accident in 2006 left Noel confined to a wheelchair and he returned to education for a newly found passion: product design.

His accident changed his perspective on life, and where previously some things were taken for granted, this was clearly no longer the case. His burning question was "How can I design for extreme circumstances too? While in the hospital I saw a lot of people struggle and I wanted to understand how I could help." He argued that innovation doesn't necessarily come from a point of pain, but rather a point of necessity. In suspect the former might create the latter or at least be a symptom of it.

For Noel, this was the new normal and things had to change in his life. After spending twenty-six years as fully able bodied, and twelve years disabled from his accident, he developed a new perspective. He went on to help hundreds of start-ups build products for millions of people, all while creating great solutions through the relevance of pain. "Looking around I have seen the difficulties that people of all abilities have and I wanted to pursue a career that might help alleviate those everyday difficulties and add value to people's lives," he shares.

This is not to say that such an unfortunate event is needed for people to gain perspective on how things work, but rather to demonstrate that innovation stems from multiple contexts. The connecting link is the way people view the world.

Can people be helped to view the world in such a way?

Absolutely! The goal of this book is to enable others to see the world through the lens of an innovator and to creatively problem solve through human-centered design. This will be achieved in the confines of co-working spaces, incubators, accelerators, start-up studios, and occasionally in larger firms too.

Tim Brown shared in *Change by Design* that "A creative team must be given the time, the space and the budget to make mistakes."[11] Large corporations are following this trend, with companies like Google or 3M being renowned for encouraging scientists and engineers to innovate by spending up to twenty percent of their time on personal experiments.

Google's Moonshot Factory, also known as Google X, is the epicenter of radical innovation. It is perhaps the only enterprise on the planet where regular investigation into the absurd is not just permitted but encouraged, and even required. Derek Thompson shares in an article how "X has quietly looked into space elevators and cold fusion. It has tried, and abandoned, projects to design hoverboards with magnetic levitation and to make affordable fuel from seawater. It has tried—and succeeded, in varying measures—to build self-driving cars, make drones that deliver aerodynamic packages, and design contact lenses that measure glucose levels in a diabetic person's tears." [12]

For some this looks like science fiction, and for others as their next project. Innovation is the concept that describes this apparent madness and that pushes humans to the edge

11 Brown, Tim. "*Change by Design: How Design Thinking Transforms Organizations and Inspires Innovation*". HarperBusiness, 2009.
12 Thompson, Derek. "Google X and the Science of Radical Creativity". *The Atlantic*, Nov. 2017. https://www.theatlantic.com/magazine/archive/2017/11/x-google-moonshot-factory/540648/.

of our creative understanding jto see what's on the other side. Every day across the world, millions of people go to work to explore just that and build, together, the future. It is our duty to support them in the best way we can.

KEY TAKEAWAYS:

- Innovation comes in many forms and sizes but nonetheless all are required for our society to progress.

- At its core, innovation is creative problem solving through elegant human-centered design.

- Innovation stems from a point of necessity, sometimes characterized by pain. As long as the need or pain is relevant to some group, a viable solution should and will be found to accommodate.

CHAPTER 2

A VERY BRIEF WALK THROUGH HISTORY

———

"What good is an idea if it remains an idea? Try. Experiment. Iterate. Fail. Try again. Change the world."

— SIMON SINEK

"The greatest glory in living lies not in never falling, but in rising every time we fall."

— NELSON MANDELA

"Remember that guy that gave up? Neither does anybody else."

— UNKNOWN

The entrepreneurial roots of the world date back to the early merchants engaged in trade thousands of years ago. Starting businesses and earning a profit from these ventures has probably been one of the longest standing jobs in human history. The concept of an entrepreneur changed its meaning as the world progressed, but it was always there to begin with. It's rooted in our DNA.

Entrepreneurship is deeply woven into the fabric of America's history. Its progress has been dependent on people producing, trading, and selling new products and services. As cited in a *Global Entrepreneurship Institute* article, Fred Bollerer, former venture partner, said, "Entrepreneurship has been going on in this country since its inception. In fact, you can say the country really started because of its political entrepreneurs."[13] A special report conducted by the *Economist* found that between 1996 and 2004 the United States created an average of 550,000 small businesses every month.[14]

For a large portion of the time, there was little innovation in the systems people used to start businesses — acknowledging

---

13 Price, Robert. "What Is the History of Entrepreneurship in America?". *Global Entrepreneurship Institute*, Nov. 9, 2015. https://news.gcase. org/2015/11/09/what-is-the-history-of-entrepreneurship-in-america/.

14 The United States of Entrepreneurs Special Report 2009. The Economist. Url: https://www.economist.com/special-report/2009/03/14/ the-united-states-of-entrepreneurs.

that, for the majority of that time, starting a business was a poorly regulated and unsupervised endeavor.

I believe that in order to understand the modern entrepreneurial space, one needs to also understand the venture capital space as those worlds are strongly intertwined.

The venture capital world started in 1946 with the creation of the American Research and Development Corporation, ARDC for short, by French-American businessman Georges Doriot. ARDC's first major success story happened when the 1957 investment of $70,000, about $630,000 in today's dollars, in Digital Equipment Corporation ended up being worth more than $38 million, about $270 million in today's dollars, at their IPO in 1966, multiplying the original investment over five hundred times -- a one hundred percent IRR for the fund.

The industry picked up speed in 1958 when "Venture Capital was in its infancy," according to Mark Heesen, former president of the National Venture Capital Association.[15] He mentions that "a significant boost was given to the industry with the passage of the Small Business Investment Act."[16]

---

15 Radler Cohen, Judy. "A Brief History of Venture Capital". Financial Poise, Nov. 21, 2018. https://www.financialpoise. com/a-brief-history-of-venture-capital/.

16 Ibid.

Up until the early 1990s, it operated as a machine to pump large sums of money into manufacturing and infrastructure businesses. After seeing the early successes of internet companies like Amazon and Netscape and their IPOs, venture capitalists ramped up investments in internet companies. The shift in direction came with little change in the actual process of investing.

In the early 2000, start-up accelerators emerged as a reaction to the disruption of the balance of power between entrepreneurs and investors when the effectiveness of venture capital firms was being questioned.[17]

In 2008, start-up guru Paul Graham wrote, "The low cost of starting a start-up means the average good bet is a riskier one, but most existing VC firms still operate as if they were investing in hardware start-ups in 1985." What he was describing was "a huge, unexploited opportunity in start-up funding: the growing disconnect between VCs, whose current business model requires them to invest large amounts, and a large class of start-ups that need less than they used to."

In 2010, he wrote that "The opportunity is a lot less unexploited now. Investors have poured into this territory from

---

17 Graham, Paul. "Why There Aren't More Googles". *Essays of Paul Graham*, Apr. 2008. http://www.paulgraham.com/googles.html.

both directions. VCs are much more likely to make angel-sized investments than they were a year ago."[18]

* * *

Nowadays, the venture world spans all countries across the world and invests in all industries and verticals. Analyzing data from CB Insights, we can see that between 2011 and 2015 the number of venture capital firms globally has grown by 15.5% each year.

The change doesn't come only in the numbers but also in the way VCs are now approaching entrepreneurial support. "As the venture industry grows and becomes more competitive and founder focused, capital alone doesn't create success stories. Here's what matters now: How the firm helps you build the community and ecosystem around your idea."[19] says Heather Hartnett, CEO and partner at Human Ventures, an early-stage venture studio in NYC that backs and builds consumer technology companies.

On the founder's side, we observe a trend of postponing IPOs across the board with many companies raising capital up to

18 Graham, Paul. "The Future of Start-up Funding". *Essays of Paul Graham*, Aug. 2010. http://www.paulgraham.com/future.html.
19 Harnett, Heather. "The Rise of "The Platform" for Venture Capital Funds". *Forbes*, Sep. 28, 2017. https://www.forbes.com/sites/heatherhartnett/2017/09/28/the-rise-of-the-platform-for-venture-capital-funds/#1def6edb4484.

series C or D. Staying private for longer means tapping VCs' increasingly deep pockets and avoiding the roller-coaster of the public markets. According to a *Morning Brew* analysis, between 1995 and 2005 the average age of a company going public was three years. Nowadays, it's eleven years.[20]

Valuations are also on the rise. When Amazon and Yahoo went public in 1997 and 1998 respectively, they were worth less than $500 million. The average valuation of VC-backed U.S. technology firms going public today is $9.6 billion, and 2019's grand total could top $150 billion.[21] Even when adjusting for inflation, the difference is stark.

This means that entrepreneurship support is in even more demand as more start-ups are being created and are holding on to their 'start-up' title for longer periods of time. This increase in founders paints a picture of a different world. For the first time, we were able to believe as a society that entrepreneurship can be taught and supported, moving away from the idea that entrepreneurs are born rather than made. This empowered more and more people to take the risk and create their own businesses.

Changes are not happening only in the venture space. The whole world is changing — and it is changing fast. We are

---

20 Morning Brew newsletter on May 10, 2019. Url: https://www.morningbrew.com/latest/archive/2019/05/10/bump/.

21 Ibid.

undergoing the Digital Revolution, probably the single greatest transformative event since the Industrial Revolution. Machine learning, AI, IoT, 5G, blockchain, among many others are changing our lives as we speak, from the way we move, to the way we live, eat, and work.

This will pose one of the hardest challenges we have faced so far: in the age of speed, how fast is too fast? As globalized nations around the world are building the technology of the future, we are struggling to keep up with all the product launches and venture deals happening. The business system as a whole is changing too.

An interesting trend is the growth of the nontraditional entrepreneurs — the independent contractor — the humble member of the gig economy. The likes of Uber, Lyft, Airbnb, Etsy, and TaskRabbit empowered this shift and many argue whether it is for the good or for the bad. The gig economy is by no means a new concept, but this past decade has seen it expand greatly.

Research showed that the share of the U.S. workforce in the gig economy rose from 10.1% in 2005 to 15.8% in 2015.[22] For many, this rapid expansion enabled new sources of revenue and created new employment opportunities. At the same time, it had major implications in the way traditional industries operated.

---

22   Katz, Lawrence and Alan Krueger. "The Rise and Nature of Alternative Work Arrangements in the United States, 1995-2015," *NBER* Working Paper No. 22667, September 2016.

The World Economic Forum reports, however, that "as most digital transformation across industries and countries continues to unfold, the *people* dimension of these transformations has emerged as the key to unlocking value and ensuring the sustainability of the changes."[23]

People start to realize that amidst all the technological change surrounding us, the human component is here to stay. We have come a long way so far. Let's keep on the right track.

KEY TAKEAWAYS:

- Historically speaking, we are producing new business at a rate we never have before. This will require a substantial infrastructure of support as we continue to innovate.

- In the middle of the Digital Revolution, the whole venture space is transforming to its core.

- One of the challenges we are facing is: In the era of speed and technology, how are we going to remain true to our human nature?

---

23 Becerra, Jorge. "The Digital Revolution Is Not About Technology – It's About People." World Economic Forum, Mar. 28, 2017. https://www.weforum.org/agenda/2017/03/the-digital-revolution-is-not-about-technology-it-s-about-people/.

CHAPTER 3

STRUGGLING TO INNOVATE

——

"If you are not embarrassed by the first version of your product, you've launched too late."

— **REID HOFFMAN**

"No company ever created a transformational growth product by asking: 'How can we do what we're already doing, a tiny bit better and a tiny bit cheaper?'"

— **MAXWELL WESSEL**

"You can't use up creativity. The more you use, the more you have."

— **MAYA ANGELOU**

Quick, when was the last time you visited a Blockbuster to rent a movie?

Unless you live in Bend, Oregon — home to the last Blockbuster on the planet -- the answer is probably too long ago for you to remember.[24]

Most of us probably know the story. Blockbuster was taken out by a little upstart DVD-by-mail business called Netflix, which has continued to innovate into streaming and now its own production studios.

Founder Reed Hastings had rented the movie *Apollo 13* and returned it well past its due date: "I had misplaced it and it was six weeks late, so it was a $40 late fee," he told 60 Minutes. "I remember 'cause I didn't want to tell my wife... I knew what she would say."[25]

On the way to the gym, he wondered why video stores didn't operate like health clubs, charging a flat membership fee. The light-bulb moment prompted Hastings to buy a bunch of DVDs and mail them to himself to see if they would travel safely through the mail.

24   Bachega, Hugo. "The Last Blockbuster: 'I'm Proud That We've Survived'." *BBC News*, Aug. 16, 2018. https://www.bbc.com/news/world-us-canada-45175194.

25   Schorn, Daniel. "The Brain Behind Netflix." *CBS News*, Dec. 01, 2006. https://www.cbsnews.com/news/the-brain-behind-netflix/.

"I opened them up, and they were fine," he said in the interview. "I thought, 'Oh my God. This is gonna work! This is gonna work!'" Hastings founded Netflix in 1997.[26]

But this didn't have to be the outcome. In the year 2000, Netflix approached Blockbuster for a buyout deal, priced at fifty million dollars. Blockbuster refused.[27]

If that decision had been reversed, you may not have to go to Bend to get your Blockbuster.

INNOVATING ON INNOVATION

The world is speeding up at an incredible rate, with the internet fueling a computing revolution on a massive scale. It is then normal to think about how this will impact the process of innovation. In recent years, we started seeing an increase in R&D expenditures along with a push for faster and more efficient processes. Companies all around the world realize the power of fast innovation systems and are racing to adapt.

26 Vozza, Stephanie . "The Random Events That Sparked 8 of the World's Biggest Start-ups." *Fast Company*, Nov. 03, 2014. https://www.fastcompany.com/3037896/the-random-events-that-sparked-8-of-the-worlds-biggest-start-ups.

27 Lucero, Diego. "Why Blockbuster Failed." *Siam Tek*. https://www.siamtek.com/why-blockbuster-failed/.

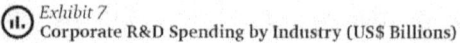

Exhibit 7
Corporate R&D Spending by Industry (US$ Billions)

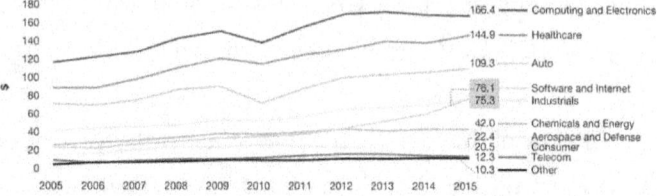

Source: Strategy& 2015 Global Innovation 1000 analysis, Bloomberg data, Capital IQ data
© 2015 PwC All rights reserved.

The software and internet industries are winning the race due to its native understanding of the technological world: one that is fast and iterative. With thousands of start-ups forming in this industry and then leveraging their products and services to disrupt others, big corporations are now forced to reconsider their aging structures in order to compete in this new arena. Some of them are determined to make radial moves to their structure and culture in order to act more like a start-up. One of the biggest problems: outrageous bureaucracy.

MOODY BLUES

In big corporations, there's an awful lot of bureaucracy and as companies get bigger, more and more people are needed to standardize processes and minimize risk. This is a normal step but will naturally slow things down as more barriers are put into place for types of deals that are out of the ordinary and could threaten profitability.

"It is hard to innovate in an existing business when you are always worried about margins," shared Keith Berry, executive director of the Moody's Analytics Accelerator.

Keith is part of a group called the Corporate Entrepreneur Community (CEC), and he shares that the topic of bureaucracy is often brought into conversation:

> "There are all these corporate gatekeepers that prevent you from doing things. When I want to partner with a start-up, the legal department is not used to make those contracts, they're usually dealing with large consulting firms. On top of that, quite often we require large insurance coverage for firms we work with and for a small start-up that might be impossible to get."

Figuring out how to work around those limitations and create exceptions to those processes is one of the keys to creating a successful corporate accelerator. When building an innovation unit inside a larger corporation, the type of sponsorship you get from higher management is really important. The mission of such a unit is to do things differently and for that to happen, exceptions have to be made. If you cannot bypass the bureaucratic process of the corporation, there is very little room for innovation and new experiments.

The problem stems from a pursuit of incremental profits and change rather than an openness to radical change that might threaten the already established flow of business. No one denies that rules and processes are there for a reason. Those gatekeepers are really there to protect the core business but in order to be relevant in today's marketplace, a company has to step outside of their comfort zone and engage in innovative activities.

What type of innovation unit would be best for your company?

Well, that is a question worth debating for a little while before diving into building one. Every company has its own needs and risks, and the innovation unit would have to address those individually. Keith talks about new corporate entrepreneurs joining the CEC and how they usually take some time to define what they are doing. It has to come naturally as a response to the question "what is the purpose of it?."

Simon Sinek would tell you to start with the "why" and he would be right.

Some companies want new sources of revenue, like Moody's Analytics did, while some want to streamline existing operations or bring new enhancements to their existing products. What works for one might not work for the other.

When deciding what type of innovation unit would be a right fit, corporations have to assess their strengths and weaknesses since they need to understand what they have to bring to the table and what they still need. We will explore this in further chapters when talking about incubators, accelerators, and start-up studios. All models described are viable as both stand alone units as well as part of a corporate entity or in partnership with one.

* * *

One drawback of large organizations is their deep desire for building consensus. Naturally, when navigating most agreements humans tend to decide in the middle, without taking any of the extreme decisions that might be needed for those "crazy" ideas to happen. With an issue so strongly rooted in the organizational DNA, it should come to no surprise the disconnect between what people think their companies should do and what they actually do.

In a report published by U.K. based PA Consulting Group, it was found that two-thirds of organizations say that innovation is crucial to survival, yet fewer than one-third say they are innovating successfully to drive growth and increase revenue.[28]

---

28 Bennett, Frazer, Anita Chandraker, Andy Katz and Hsiu Mei Wong. "Innovation Matters." *PA Consulting*, 2016. https://www.paconsulting. com/insights/2016/innovation-matters/.

On top of that, more than three-fifths of senior executives feel that CEOs are not leading from the front and lack the vision and passion needed to make innovation happen. With only a quarter of U.K. organizations saying their boards put a priority on innovation, but two-fifths of U.K. leaders rejecting disruptive ideas for fear of failure, it is no surprise that more and more companies have been looking towards start-ups and innovation units as a possible solution to those problems.

But are they the solution?

ISSUES AT THOMSON

Thomson CompuMark, a subsidiary of Thomson Reuters Corporation, is a business unit that has been around for decades in a very traditional business space. They are providing trademark research and brand protection solutions, or "homework for trademark attorneys," as John Schloff puts it, a former senior director of product management.

In other words, they are helping trademark attorneys who work for clients who want a name for their new product and are interested in establishing a formal legal ownership of that name. They do the research for the attorneys and thus help them make informed decisions. The legal industry as a whole is very risk averse and will take every chance the lawyers have to further reduce their risk. CompuMark is providing the detailed data analysis that is needed to make sure it's safe to establish the name as a new trademark.

How they do it?

You see, the delivery of the service has been the same for years. We are discussing human based services after all. You have analysts, some of them who have been on staff for years and years, working to analyze data and provide insights. No matter how many sophisticated internal tools they are using, the human component has been an integral part of the service being offered.

The issue with this?

An entrant to the market, a start-up that hopes to digitally disrupt the industry and change the workflow of the process. Instead of having a client contracting human based services, they developed a platform in which the user can key in the word they want and the system would do the analysis for them. A digital solution that can provide the client with ratings and suggestions about the quality and risk level of the trademark — all through the click of a button.

Thomson Reuters saw this issue on the horizon for a while, but didn't decide to take charge of it until now.

John mentioned that when there is potential for digital disruption to happen, it's always better to disrupt your own business than to have someone else disrupt it. Disruption can be crazy, and it often involves massive amounts of change on many levels and across different departments, especially when you have a lot of stiff infrastructure built in the space. It becomes dangerous to tip yourself over, but never as dangerous as having someone else do that to you.

* * *

As John recalls, they started working on establishing a more reliable digital solution, in part as a response to this start-up. Risk was still the main point of concern among the trademark attorneys and this platform couldn't guarantee the same reliability as their human based competitors could. A *Forbes* article mentions risk aversion as one of the key factors preventing large corporations from driving innovation.[29] The author puts it nicely when he says that "Managing to quarterly earnings reports where companies are crucified for missing their forecasted earnings by as little as one penny per share, sending their stock prices tumbling, is the key driver here."[30]

---

29 Deeb, George. "The 5 Reasons Big Companies Struggle With Innovation." *Forbes*, Jan. 8, 2014. https://www.forbes.com/sites/georgedeeb/2014/01/08/the-five-reasons-big-companies-struggle-with-innovation/#31d697702958.

30 Ibid.

Thomson Reuters saw an opportunity to innovate and bring the ease of a digital product with the security of an aged, but fully functioning, human based process. After all, clients have been working with them for years because of the trust they built around the data they provided. It drove them to make informed decisions and properly manage the risk for their subsequent clients. The challenge now was to design a product that would be able to integrate the advantages of speed and usability, with the excellence required to maintain the clients' trust levels. After all, no one wants to wait a couple of days for a human to answer to an email with a solution.

It's been four years since John left the company, but they were able to develop something really thorough that can assure the attorneys of the reliability of the outputs. The workflow didn't change too much, but the algorithms are clearly getting better and better.

The expectation for the future: revenue starts moving towards the software-backed solutions as the company fully transitions into the new digital chapter.

Companies that are not able to constantly innovate and are not sufficiently responsive to the market will, in the long run, go out of business, no matter their current situation. As John mentioned in our interview, there are two main challenges a large enterprise is facing when trying to move as quickly as a start-up. The first one is the culture. Take the example of Pitney Bowes, a company that focused primarily on one industry for almost one hundred years, recently expanding into e-commerce, software, and other technologies. A culture that is formed over the course of many decades is very hard, if not impossible, to change. In the case of Pitney Bowes, bringing alternatives that fly in the face of the culture is a difficult process but when paired with a market push in that direction, the solution seems clear no matter the pains of change.

The second issue is the existing infrastructure and workflow. When an organization has been delivering products and services in an industry for a period of time, they amass methodologies, processes, infrastructure, and trained employees. On top of that, they secure revenue streams and develop optimized cost structures. The work becomes easier and more profitable. All of that is at risk of change due to a digital disruption. In the case of Thomson Reuters, the services provided for the attorneys were built on value and trust. When they began exploring the digital solutions to deliver the same value, their cost structure changed dramatically which the clients realized.

Now, why would they be willing to pay the same premium if the work became cheaper and easier on the other end? The market was now pushing back to lower the price of the services. When you have the financial flows associated with certain services under the risk of change, disruption seems even harder, but nonetheless required for progress.

We can see that there are many factors influencing the ability of organizations to innovate, and the larger the company the more prevalent those problems are. When comparing companies like Apple, Amazon, Google, Facebook, and IBM to others such as Blockbuster Video, American Motors, Kodak, and Pan Am Airlines, one can realize that without a proper infrastructure for innovation to happen, failure is bound to occur.

KEY TAKEAWAYS:

- Innovation is critical for the success of a company.

- Software and technology industries are the best positioned to take advantage of R&D driven innovation and increased expenditures can be observed.

- The tendency to gravitate towards the middle prevents managers and employees from approaching "wild ideas" that are necessary for innovation to occur.

- The risk aversion that comes with performance tied to financial metrics is an important factor to consider when designing innovation frameworks, as it may prevent the ability to try new projects.

PART II

THE HUMAN APPROACH IN THEORY

CHAPTER 4

DIVERSITY & INCLUSION

——

"It is time for parents to teach young people early on that in diversity there is beauty and there is strength."

— *MAYA ANGELOU*

"A diverse mix of voices leads to better discussions, decisions, and outcomes for everyone."

— *SUNDAR PICHAI, CEO OF GOOGLE*

Leanne Robers has been an entrepreneur three times so far in her life, but every time was for a new reason and posed different challenges.

The first time was intentional. She wanted to have something that she could call her own. Back then there was less of a race towards entrepreneurship, but rather an aspiration to build businesses. Leanne and her business partner started a lifestyle company that built and managed boutique hotels and F&B outlets. The journey was harder than expected. and three years later she left due to a conflict with the other founder.

The second time was accidental. Leanne was in business school and as a highly skilled professional, multiple colleagues were asking her to join their new ventures. "I was reluctant after the first attempt, it was hard for me to give in," she shares. A compromise was reached as Leanne was able to work as a consultant for multiple ventures which reopened her appetite for entrepreneurship. With one in particular, she felt she was working so closely with the project that she was basically one of the entrepreneurs. With more and more energy involved, she ended up joining them as the CEO of The Hedge Club, a company set to connect budding fund managers with retail investors in an unbiased marketplace by showcasing manager's investment performance and publishing it on social media to attract investment capital.

The third time was even more serendipitous. Leanne and her friend realized that they are complementing each other very well and that working together on a project might be a great experience. Up until that point, they just hadn't had the chance to do so. Leanne Robers and Kevin Larken met in the picturesque city of Jakarta, Indonesia, a place brimming with artistic talent. Leanne wanted to help her talented and creative aunt who had been struggling for twenty years to sell her artwork. She, like many other creators in Southeast Asia, had trouble getting visibility and recognition. Kevin, who worked with buyers in Asia for over a decade, knew that the best work was always a collaborative effort - but successful collaboration was extremely difficult to achieve.

"It was in a casual conversation at a restaurant when realized there was a gap in the market that could be filled by us: to unleash creativity in the world, creators and buyers need a new way to come together - a simpler, guided way." In 2015, Comish, a peer-to-peer art commissioning platform, was born.

FROM FOUNDER TO SUPPORTER

Leanne is an amazing example of a fearless woman entrepreneur, but her resume doesn't end there. She took the role to help empower and support other women who are embarking on this journey. Originally the head of Singapore and now a general partner for She Loves Tech, Leanne is helping female founders with a passion. She is managing all operations outside of China for the world's largest entrepreneurial support unit for women in technology. Her work focuses on building and developing sponsorship and partnerships for their programs, the backbone of this not-for-profit organization. Currently present in sixteen international locations, they are planning to expand to over twenty locations next year, touching every single continent.

The problem is not that there aren't enough women interested in starting technology businesses, but rather that when they do show interest women are given little funding, resources, and support. There are many reasons for why this is happening. A primary reason is the lack of gender diversity among venture capitalists. It is well known that people have this basic tendency to associate with people who are similar to them. When talking about business this bias grows exponentially, as we see over and over again with investors trusting their money to people who are similar to them.

So what do we do when there is this imbalance between the investor size and the entrepreneurial one? You're joining a quest to increase awareness about the biases people bring to the table, but that's not always easy.

Leanne recalls being in meetings trying to raise funds for Comish and having investors not even look her in the eyes despite being the CEO of the company. Her male co-founder was the target of all questions, and even if she would be the one answering it investors would follow up with him afterwards. While this truly baffled me, in reality this occurs in so many boardrooms across North America. We need to make sure all stakeholders understand that the start-up needs those individuals. In the case of Comish, it was Kevin who headed the product development but Leanne managed all other business aspects. One without the other could have not built the start-up it needed them both to survive.

DATA-DRIVEN REALITY CHECK

In an interview with Ryan Kushner, Sandra Kwak, CEO of 10Power, shared the following: "Despite the fact that women-led businesses are the fastest growing sector in US entrepreneurship, the odds are stacked against women raising venture capital. Fortune reported that women received 2% of venture capital in 2017, while Inc. in 2018 illuminated an even deeper chasm faced by women of color, who received only 0.2% of VC dollars. This is distressing, especially considering that diversity improves portfolio performance: companies with a female founder outperformed all-male founding teams by 63% according to First Round data. Between 2007 and 2016, there were 2.8 million new firms launched by women of color and nearly 8 out of 10 new woman-owned enterprises have a founder of color. The lack of representation in VC firms plays a large role, entrenching patterns of exclusion through unconscious bias."

In 2017, *Harvard Business Review* reported that "Firms with a female partner are more than twice as likely as firms without a female partner to invest in a company with a woman on the management team (34% vs 13%); and they are three times as likely to invest in women CEOs (58% vs 15%)."[31]

I'm wondering, with all this data available, how can we still fall in such old mindsets and make the same mistakes over and over again when deciding who to invest in and bring into our team? One should be able to recognize those biases and make decisions based on facts, rather than their subjective point of view.

Entrepreneurial support units are now pushed to think more broadly and understand that product development will always be more efficient and yield better results when everyone is allowed to sit at the table.

At the same time, we need to make sure we are designing resources that lower the barrier to entry for all groups of people, especially the less represented groups. The investor side is only half of the story. It is not just access to money that's

---

31   DuBow, Wendy and Allison-Scott Pruitt. "The Comprehensive Case for Investing More VC Money in Women-Led Startups". *Harvard Business Review*, Sep. 18, 2017. https://hbr.org/2017/09/the-comprehensive-case-for-investing-more-vc-money-in-women-led-startups.

stopping some from becoming entrepreneurs, but the lack of proper dedicated support from early stage to scaling or exit.

When looking at entrepreneurial support units in North America, research performed by JP Morgan's analysts shows that 69% have no special focus on the type of people they are targeting.[32] The rest have either one or more, with 9% focusing on women, 8% on African-Americans, 6% on low-income entrepreneurs, and 3% on non-US citizens.[33] This is clearly a beginning for change to occur, but the reality is that access to entrepreneurship resources is still not equitable across all segments of the population.

STUDENT-DRIVEN INNOVATION

Julia Maddox, director of the Barbara J. Burger iZone, the student innovation hub at the University of Rochester, talked about the importance of putting the experts in the driver's seat.

Let the product development to be driven by the consumers and led by people close to them. It is incredible to see how many assumptions people make when designing for

---

32 JPMorgan Chase & Co. and ICIC Report. "Creating Inclusive High-Tech Incubators and Accelerators: Strategies to Increase Participation Rates Women and Minority Entrepreneurs". 2016.

33 Ibid.

someone else. When the product team looks nothing like your consumer, you are on track to an increased chance of failure. But when a product team partners with their users directly they're able to find insights that wouldn't otherwise be obvious. The founders of Aribnb are one of the many examples available.

At iZone, this user-centered mindset is truly embraced. Since this is an innovation hub at a university, it should follow naturally that students are best at recognizing their own problems and designing programs that will help them. As such, a team of student employees leads most of iZone's programming. With a very diverse student body, comes a very diverse and active team as well.

"It is incredibly important to put the experts in those positions not in a patronizing way, but in a way that acknowledges that they know best what is valuable for their peers," she shares.

Her approach pays off with hundreds of students being impacted by the iZone programming on a monthly basis.

In his bestselling book, *Change by Design*, Tim Brown mentions how "There is a popular saying around IDEO that all of us are smarter than any of us, and this is the key to unlocking the creative power of any organization,"[34] One should not add people to a team just for the sake of diversity, but rather be mindful of the users and do their best at representing them on the creator side.

Is there a recipe for this?

Julia mentions that "If I hired 10 people that looked like me, extroverted, running around and aggressively chasing ideas and new projects, we wouldn't have had most of our great rituals and programming, nor the same execution capacity. I need people around me to challenge me and tell me when I'm wrong. We need this diverse pool of people to be relevant."

Without a doubt, different perspectives, educational backgrounds, and experiences facilitate the exploratory competence of a firm through more efficient problem solving and increased output of novel ideas.[35]

She continues to share, "We are a space for everybody and our staffing has to reflect that. Fundamentally, it will empower us to come up with more creative ideas, because we will be able to build on top of each other's."

---

34 Brown, Tim. *Change by Design: How Design Thinking Transforms Organizations and Inspires Innovation.* HarperBusiness, 2009.

35 Quintana-García, Cristina and Carlos Benavides-Velasco. "*Innovative Competence, Exploration and Exploitation: The Influence of Technological Diversification*". Research Policy 37, (2008): 492-507.

RESEARCH DILEMMA

As a start-up support unit, it is crucial to empower your founders to think strategically about the diversity of their teams and the relevance to the end user. When making hiring decisions, they'll have to consider who will be able to best represent the customers and who will be able to challenge the status quo and drive real innovation. People have this preconceived notion that hiring for diversity is an alternative to hiring for performance, but fail to ask if they are defining "most talented" and "most qualified" correctly. I would argue that you will be able to find incredible talent in any place, no matter their gender, race, nationality, age, ability status, or socioeconomic status.

Recent research by London School of Economics professor Max Nathan and University of Lancaster professor Neil Lee shows that "companies with diverse management are more likely to introduce new product innovations than are those with homogeneous top teams,"[36] proving that diversity is both an economic asset as well as a social benefit.

More current research paints an increasingly complex story of the issue where different types of diversity are considered and the area of impact varies. Chinesee researchers

---

36   Nathan, Max and Neil Lee. *"Cultural Diversity, Innovation, And Entrepreneurship: Firm-level Evidence From London"*. Economic Geography 89, no. 4 (2013): 367-394.

Ramasamy and Yeung find that ethnically homogeneous but value-diverse countries are the best at innovation. Others seem to agree that not all measurements of diversity hold equal weight in the race for the next revolutionary new product or service.[37]

A Danish-Icelandic research trio performed an analysis of a large scale study of 1,775 managers of danish companies and found out that there is a positive relation between diversity in education and gender and the likelihood of introducing innovative products. Interestingly, they found no significant effect of ethnical diversity on the firm's likelihood to innovate.[38]

Even with this in mind, it is important to understand that diversity approached from a more meta perspective is without a doubt a foundational step towards innovation. But if we truly want to change the entrepreneurial scene and make it more equitable for all, that change has to come from all stakeholders.

One interesting example is the one of 37 Angels, an angel investment fund founded by Angela Lee, the CIO of Columbia Business School. She created it "as the network I would have wanted to pitch when I was a founder, and also as an

37 Ramasamy, Bala and Matthew Yeung. *"Diversity and Innovation"*. Applied Economics Letters 23, no. 14 (2016): 1037–1041.

38 Østergaard, Christian, Bram Timmermans and Kari Kristinsson. *"Does a different view create something new? The effect of employee diversity on innovation"*. Research Policy 40, no. 3 (2011): 500-509.

angel network I wanted to be a part of as an investor. We have a 1-month in-person boot camp, and an 8-week online boot camp that activates new investors by taking them through the entire deal flow process."[39] Their model has education as one of the core pillars, with continual learning on the investor side being the norm. Apart from their formal programs, they host monthly lunches and learn where they cover relevant topics.

Most of the time, making investors aware of what is going on and how the world is changing is the first step in the right direction. We cannot expect everyone to be as open minded as we would want them to be, but assuming that every person can change and grow will empower us to educate more people and thus make the entrepreneurial scene more equitable for all.

KEY TAKEAWAYS:

- Successful entrepreneurial support units understand that innovation sparks from diversity, and unless everyone is at the table where product development decisions are made, a significant share of customers will be ignored.

---

39 Kushner, Ryan. *Accelerate This!: A Super Not Boring Guide To Startup Accelerators And Clean Energy Entrepreneurship*. CreateSpace Independent Publishing Platform, 2018.

- In order to stay relevant, they will have to both attract a diverse pool of founders and inspire them to develop diverse leadership and product teams.

- Training the investor side of the equation on the benefits of diversity is equally important as it is to have diversity among the entrepreneurs they are supporting.

- There is still some debate about whether all aspects of one's identity hold the same weight in the optimal diversity mix that's conducive to innovation.

CHAPTER 5

NETWORKS, MENTORS & PARTNERS

"It is the long history of humankind (and animal kind, too) that those who learned to collaborate and improvise most effectively have prevailed."

— *CHARLES DARWIN*

"We make a living by what we get, we make a life by what we give."

— SIR WINSTON CHURCHILL

"Lack of direction, not lack of time, is the problem. We all have twenty-four hour days."

— ZIG ZIGLAR

One of the first clients of consulting firm K&J Growth was the University of Delaware. They needed help with their start-up competition for high schoolers. More specifically, they wanted at least five hundred business to submit an application. The deadline: two weeks away. So, how do you get five hundred teams to join a start-up competition? K&J put on their creative hats and went straight to work. University of Delaware reached out to the community and hoped for the best.

The team, on the other hand, decided to run an integrated marketing campaign and fight on multiple fronts. They got a list of students and ran an email campaign, set up a giveaway, and reached out to influencers for shoutouts. Everything was going less than amazing, until they decided that building an audience from scratch might not be the best solution. They aggressively focused their creative marketing endeavors to tap into community builders and get them to spread the message to their audience. With the right mindset and everyone putting time and effort into promotion, they were able to leverage their connections and get 859 applicants, surpassing the initial goal by almost double. Tapping into existing communities by strategically forming partnerships magnified the result of the marketing campaign. When trying to replicate what K&J did, the caveat is to make sure the partnership is mutually beneficial.

It is not rocket science to figure out that when others have put the work to create communities, accessing them instead of building one from scratch is more efficient. Entrepreneurial support units, through their network and years of operation, naturally receive access to several communities and those privileges get passed down to their founders. In a world more connected than ever, it is important for such units to cultivate relationships with a number of stakeholders in order to achieve that connection.

Interestingly, units who are based in smaller cities with less competition for support services have a higher chance of tapping into existing communities because of their increased brand awareness among the people around them. Most of the time though, that market is too small for founders to get an incredible competitive advantage, but serves perfectly as a launch ramp towards bigger pies. For small and medium businesses who intend to stay local, that access is everything they need in order to reach a majority of their customers. It is up to the support unit to decide how much support they can actually offer and to what scale their network and partnership possibilities lay.

The power of those connections is sometimes overlooked in favor of more "practical" resources such as office space, discounted software and services, or top tier educational materials. For a founder who doesn't have an extensive network and is trying to strike those deals on their own, it sometimes depends on good fortune and luck to stumble across them. Even when that is the case, it is a mere bias to think that in the long term those seemingly practical resources hold more value than a well-connected program in a thriving ecosystem.

* * *

Sometimes, a unit may not even be necessary for those connections to happen. This is the case of Jonathan Maxim, the co-founder and CEO of Vea Fitness, a company that rewards people for staying active. He built an app that lets the user select a challenge then walk, run, or bike it in order to be eligible for a discount from a partner company. A two mile run could get you 10% of athletic apparel and if you're ready to go one more, you might be surprised by a 5% increase.

After successfully launching the app with individuals, Jonathan started looking for B2B opportunities such as targeting companies who want to get their employees to work out. Trying to find creative ways to reach those businesses, he stumbled across an unexpected but amazing opportunity as he was working on a partnership with Snap Kitchen, a start-up that sells pre-made meals under subscription service. He recalls being in one of their restaurants pitching his idea to the cashier who agreed to introduce him to the marketing manager.

Little did he know that the woman was also organizing an event with the city of Philadelphia later that month. She bought into the idea, and beyond the partnership she offered him a spot as one of the sponsors of the event if they give the runners free access to their platform. We are not talking about any event, we are talking big scale — very big scale, like multiple-closed-streets-and-over-a-thousand-runners type of big. Needless to say, he accepted the offer. The city started running billboards around the area and all bus stations had banners about the event.

What was also on them?

You might have guessed: Vea Fitness logo. After doing the math, that happy encounter brought Jonathan and his team over $100,000 worth of marketing. The trade was a major success, and their app was getting thousands of downloads during the event. A creative partnership gave them access to a bigger network than they expected at that point. All through the power of networking combined with a little luck. You know how they say, "you have to be at the right place at the right time."

FROM STRANGER TO MENTOR TO CO-FOUNDER

Jason Ford is the current vice president of software engineering at house printing company ICON3D and partner in the Saturn V start-up studio. He was living in Memphis when he started working in technology and media. There he met a guy around twenty years older than him who was working at a company he wanted to work for. Jason invited the man to have lunch and during the conversation he received advice to move to Austin. Reluctant in the beginning, he ended up making the decision to move and never regretted it.

Once there he met another man who he worked with at a company in Austin. The individual, who was ten years older and held a more senior position, decided to take a new role at another company that Jason admired. He recalls, "I wanted to work at his new place and hoped to get him to help me secure that position, but during our conversation he said that he thinks I should be an entrepreneur and this is the reason why I am bored at my current job." So in 2009 he ended up starting a company called Feedmagnet and began seeking out advice from people who went through the process of founding a start-up. He remembers being at a networking event after a demo day. Jason didn't know anyone there, but wanted to hear the pitches.

He recalls how "At lunch, I wanted to get the attention of more experienced people who looked like they knew what they were doing. One older guy seemed to fit the profile so I sat down next to him and struck up a conversation. Turns out that he ran the biggest VC fund in Austin and then started a company, took it public and eventually merged it with IBM. I was blown away. He seemed interested in my work so we started to grab coffee every couple months and then once a month and then once or twice a week and out of a sudden he becomes one of my closest mentors. One day he asks me if he can work for me. I was shocked. Why would he work for me? work doing what?! He suggested being the COO, but I thought to myself "If you end up working for me you should be the CEO" so that's what we did and I became the president. He basically moved from advising me to advising the whole company. He was very hard to impress and that kept me going back to the drawing board over and over again. He helped me grow the company and sell it to Bazaarvoice in 2014. I wouldn't have pulled it off without him."

SERENDIPITY

Entrepreneurial support units are a prime spot for those strategic connections to happen. Jonathan Maxim realized his team needed to be around people that could foster a community of mutual aid. After being part of different co-working spaces and incubators, he realized that the community is what truly makes them different. Resources are secondary. The networking and connection opportunities are what set them apart.

He now runs his own company from the comfort of his home, but takes on every chance to go to coffee shops and stay connected. His personal connections earned him access to high caliber people which greatly helped his business. "When I was running Vea Fitness in an accelerator I got introduced to most new users and influencers that could get my brand out there. I even got the chance to connect with Kevin Hart, Ashton Kutcher and Kanye West."

Apparently, some of the people Jonathan was with in the co-working space knew one of Kevin Hart's friends. They were running a music agency business and wanted to host a party, so Jonathan offered his house for the location. They brought the guy to the event and he came with no one else but Kevin Hart himself. Good music, some cocktails, proper networking, and the talent manager promised Jonathan an introduction to Kevin. You could feel the excitement of the situation as he ended up investing in Vea Fitness and Jonathan worked with him for a year-and-a-half.

The adventure doesn't stop there.

During that period, he was able to get introductions to Ashton Kutcher and Kanye West, having them become part of the story. It sometimes may seem impossible to make those high profile connections, but it is important to note that there is something inside of all of us that excites us when we see a great opportunity, no matter our wealth or fame. Those people have a drive to be entrepreneurial too and when they can be part of something cool, equity included, they jump straight in. It all starts with an introduction and a handshake.

* * *

While sometimes planned, most encounters of this type are mere acts of serendipity. One could argue that if that is the case, entrepreneurial support units do not add much value into fostering the development of such relationships.

In the same manner, if I would ask you whether you would want to bet on one side of a fair coin or one side of a fair dice, you would pick the coin every time — the probabilities of those encounters are not the same in all situations. No matter the aspect of chance, dedicated programs and events around the world have the responsibility and resources necessary to make "serendipity" happen more often.

Heather Hartnett shares that "At Human Ventures, for example, we made a deliberate decision to build a "Human Network" that functions to support three key areas: engaging and developing founder relationships, building early stage teams, and connecting startups with an extended network of experts, early adopters, and customers."[40]

---

40 Harnett, Heather. "The Rise of "The Platform" for Venture Capital Funds". *Forbes*, Sep. 28, 2017. https://www.forbes.com/sites/heatherhartnett/2017/09/28/the-rise-of-the-platform-for-venture-capital-funds/#1def6edb4484.

Mike Lightman, managing partner at Big Idea Ventures, argues that "fundamentally, coaching and mentoring are probably two of the biggest value-add items that exist in an entrepreneurial support program. Everything else is kind of the icing on the cake." The mingling among founders gives them the opportunity to meet with potential suppliers, share wisdom, close deals, and potentially raise money.

It is not only about connecting people in the network through community events and access to contact databases, but also providing organized mentorship programming for the specific verticals the unit is operating in. "The key to real business development support is not to provide speed dating opportunities between corporations and startups, but to actually curate a real discussion that is relevant to both parties' strategic goals,"[41] says Maria Palma, Director of Platform at RRE Ventures. In today's business environment, this has become a requirement rather than a differentiating factor.

This has been observed across the board including in venture capital firms. "Designated network and event managers at venture capital firms are becoming increasingly common as investors see knowledge sharing as a way to support new and existing founders, stimulate referrals, create business

41   Ibid.

development opportunities and fuel deal flow."[42] shares Stephanie Manning, director of platform at Lerer Hippeau, a venture capital firm based in New York City, in a *Forbes* article.

A 2017 study using a longitudinal field experiment found that even in a college setting, an entrepreneur-mentor increases the likelihood of joining or founding a start-up.[43] The results hold true for non-university-affiliated programs too, with the entrepreneur-mentor effect being significantly stronger for people whose parents were not entrepreneurs.[44] A guiding figure is necessary for those founders, no matter how young, to navigate the intricacies of starting a business. Mentors can also help question the founder's assumptions and thus drive more robust product development.

While researching this subject, I was curious to see if those mentor relationships are equally effective across cultures. Through my journeys in the United States, Europe, and East Asia, I asked incubator and accelerator managers the same question: How does mentorship look like here? Almost

---

42 Manning, Stephanie. "Why VC Firms Are Investing In Platform To Compete". *Forbes*, May 8, 2019. https://www.forbes.com/sites/valleyvoices/2019/05/08/why-vc-firms-are-investing-in-platform/#507300342b94.

43 Eesley, Charles and Yanbo Wang. "*Social Influence In Career Choice: Evidence From A Randomized Field Experiment On Entrepreneurial Mentorship*". Research Policy 46, no. 3 (2017): 636-650.

44 Ibid.

unanimously, they described a process of pairing founders with people who are experienced in that particular industry in order to assist them. Even though cultural differences exist in how comfortable people are asking for help, the need for the help needlessly exists and is not to be ignored.

In the United States and Europe, great importance is placed on the skills and track record of mentors. This is a consequence of the societal design of the capitalist Western world. Care should be taken though when selecting mentors, even those with a brilliant track record. Just because someone is successful doesn't make them a great mentor. Some are incapable of explaining why they were successful and cannot teach nor empathize with the mentee.

In East Asian countries, the focus is more on the perceived intention of the mentor. A recent study showed that among Chinese founders the intention of the mentor is the strongest predictor of the success of the relationship, as it lays the foundation for the development of the interactive dynamic between the mentor and the mentee.[45] The intention of the mentee seemed to be less impactful on the rate of success, creating an unbalanced influence.[46]

---

45   Ting, Song Xiao, Liu Feng, and Wang Qin. "*The Effect of Entrepreneur Mentoring and its Determinants in the Chinese Context*". Management Decision 55, no. 7 (2017): 1410-1425.

46   Ibid.

We need to start thinking about incubators and accelerators as platforms, not as a process. Many transactions completed inside are non-financial, such as mentorship. The reason why mentors come to those programs varies, but these relationships are always a two-way stream of knowledge.

SUPER-MENTORING

Fostering a network of talented individuals that entrepreneurs can tap into when needed is crucial for successful support units. This is something that is universally found across all types of organizations, no matter their structure. The most powerful ones are able to get top tier experts to serve as mentors. It is also important to note that geographical proximity is not a requirement anymore in the digital age, but sometimes the accessibility that comes with having people in the same space or the same city increases the chances of those meaningful connections to happen. Afterall, the in-person interaction will always build stronger relationships.

With those stronger relationships, more benefits come. Eric Koester, Georgetown University professor and founder of the Creator Institute, argues that "people don't need mentors, they need super-mentors — who can offer not just advice but access to networks."

When I began working on my second start-up, I was in dire need of advice and support. The reality was: I wasn't really sure of what I was doing. Through the entrepreneurship center, I got connected with a couple of entrepreneurs in residence (EIRs). With some, it was only a thirty minute conversation. With others, great relationships evolved. One of them in particular led to a myriad of opportunities even after I stepped down from my role at the start-up. That was the super-mentor relationship that Eric was talking about. Founders need access to networks so they can ask questions and run ideas by others. Support programs are best equipped to be the center of gravity of this network effect: with more founders coming in and graduating from the program, the more valuable the system becomes.

KEY TAKEAWAYS:

- The development of partnerships, seemingly random at first, is greatly supported by entrepreneurial programs.

- Effective support programs have a strong network that is aligned with the verticals of operation and is accessible to founders.

- Mentorship programs have to focus on distributing access to one's network rather than just providing advice.

CHAPTER 6

EMPATHY, CULTURE & SUCCESS

———

"Culture eats strategy for breakfast."

- PETER DRUCKER

"When you show deep empathy toward others, their defensive energy goes down, and positive energy replaces it. That's when you can get more creative in solving problems."

- STEPHEN COVEY

"Being a great place to work is the difference between being a good company and a great company."

- BRIAN KRISTOFEK

Jeff Slobotski and Dusty Davidson started working on Big Omaha ten years ago — an annual conference that brings founders, supporters, and investors together in Nebraska. The first conference took place in May 2009 at Kaneko in the Old Market of Omaha. Over the years they learned that the most important thing a community builder can do is listen to the people comprising that community. Sounds a little obvious, but riding the wave of success can sometimes come with an unintentional blindness to the obvious.

For a while, everything was going incredibly well and tickets sold out in a matter of days. Big Omaha became what the name suggested: the big event in Omaha. The next logical step was, of course, adding more events and growing the conference even more. Their crazy move was to add part of the program not in another neighborhood but in an entirely different city, Kansas City.

So how do you get folks between those locations in the same day?

It was a logistical nightmare and a clear stretch for even the most innovative of people. More importantly, Big Omaha was a local pride, being supported by the people from the eastern Nebraska city. The community did not expand all the way to Kansas City.

So how can you expand without losing that local feeling?

It is hard to do when the geographical nearness is one of the core aspects of the conference. The duo ended up giving up the Kansas City expansion for that very reason. Soon after, in 2015 the conference was bought by AIM, a not-for-profit organization that promotes technology to empower people, enhance organizations, and create brilliant communities.

Brian Lee, the managing director of the new parent organization, when asked about expansion plans said, "Our goal is not to outgrow Kaneko. We want to preserve the charm and the experience (of Big Omaha) for as long as we can."[47]

The lesson learned for Jeff and his team: make sure you listen to the community and provide them with what they want. Pushing too much on them, even though it might seem like the great next step, could not be the best move. The culture of an event is equally as important, if not even more, than the offerings and size. That was not the only lesson they learned by putting Big Omaha together.

If you go on Jeff's personal website, you will see a reference from the one and only Zappos founder and CEO, Tony

---

47 Townley, Wendy. "Big Omaha: Bringing Together Designers, Tech Giants, Startups, and Investors". *Omaha Magazine*, May 24, 2017. https://omahamagazine.com/articles/big-omaha/.

Hsieh. Asked how he met the legend, he smiled and said "Big Omaha."

The two had some mutual friends in the start-up community for a number of years, but it was when Tony agreed to come and speak at the event that the two properly connected. Tony had a great time at the event and they were able to keep in touch afterwards and slowly transform the business relationship into a real friendship. How? Jeff recalls, "You have to always think of ways you can be helpful to others. Tony is a great believer in building start-up communities outside of traditional cities. The question naturally became: how can I help him? I want to do business and help other good humans."

Empathy is key at succeeding in life and business.

No matter where you are or what you are doing, no matter how many or few resources you have available, find ways to listen and be helpful. Be able to build on top of what you have and add value to others. Empathy drives great cultures. Empathy drives great relationships.

Julia Maddox shares about the Barbara J. Burger iZone innovation hub that "The culture that we are setting up here doesn't exist in a vacuum. We have to practice what we preach and use all our tools to challenge the status quo. We are a space that feels inherently creative, there are clues everywhere that something is happening here, but this has to be organic — a symptom of your culture. Empathy sits at the core of all of this."

THEIR CULTURE OR OURS?

Since an entrepreneurial support unit is an organization giving birth to other organizations, there are multiple cultures evolving at the same time. But how can we cultivate empathy in the entrepreneurs we are supporting? Logically, one could say lead by the power of example but that is not enough. Even though we ourselves have to lead the units with empathy, an open conversation about the way founders approach relationship building is necessary. We have to tactically assist them in designing positive cultures for their forthcoming businesses.

But what exactly is a culture?

Gary Vaynerchuck, the famous entrepreneur and social media influencer, shared in a Tweet that "if you think about business like a computer, culture is the operating system. Everything else is an "app." Finance is an app. Creative is an app. Strategy is an app. But culture is the operating system."

In a more rigorous explanation, organizational culture is defined as the collection of employees' perceptions about the organization, its values, norms, and their expectations surrounding it.[48] Its importance spans all key performance indicators of the company and even mediates the link between performance measurement and job satisfaction, employee retention, and self-reported performance.[49] The relation describes a requirement for a positive organizational culture in order to be able to predict the level of job satisfaction from individual performance.[50] In other words, in a positive work environment productive employees typically enjoy their work, stay at the company longer, and evaluate themselves more accurately. It has been observed that strong, positive cultures energize employees and boost performance, leveraging values and norms to shift the attention towards key organizational priorities.[51]

Small alterations to the design of work can produce meaningful changes in the long term. For example, in recent years it has become more and more important to integrate positive psychology concepts into the workplace as millennials are

---

48 Gibson, James, John Ivancevich, James Donnelly and Robert Konopaske. *"Organizations: Behavior, Structure, Processes"*. McGraw-Hill, 2012.

49 Cravens, Karen, Elizabeth Goad Oliver, Shigehiro Oishi and Jeanine Stewart. *"Workplace Culture Mediates Performance Appraisal Effectiveness and Employee Outcomes: A Study in a Retail Setting"*. Journal of Management Accounting Research 27, no. 2 (2015): 1–34.

50 Ibid.

51 Chatman, Jennifer and Sandra Eunyoung Cha. *"Leading by Leveraging Culture"*. California Management Review 45, no. 4 (2003): 20–34.

seen to pay closer attention to their self-concepts, personal relationships, and work relationships.[52]

As the border between work and personal life shrinks, younger employees are looking for more meaning in their jobs and work environments that match their values and ideals in life. Essentially, people want to work with people they want to be around not just in a work setting but also in a social setting, because they are assessing their own image of the self through their employment situation. This requires an organizational focus on ethical behavior in order to promote healthy and positive images of the self among employees and attract like-minded people in the firm.

* * *

So is it worth investing the time and energy into such design work? Research seems to say yes.

Researchers Ganster from Colorado State University and Rosen from the University of Arkansas showed that more positive social behavior will naturally lead to reduced stress and subsequently to reduced anxiety and improved job

---

52 Graen, George and Miriam Grace. "*Positive Industrial and Orga-nizational Psychology: Designing for Tech-Savvy, Optimistic, and Purposeful Millennial Professionals' Company Cultures*". Industrial and Organizational Psychology 8, no. 3 (2015): 395-408.

attitudes.[53] Another recent study, this time from the University of California, shows that happy employees are more likely to be successful in their careers.[54] The two researchers, Boehm and Lyubomirsky, found out that happy employees perform better on their tasks and report greater satisfaction at work.[55] This translates into an increase in productivity and a smaller chance of failure. Moreover, other studies show that positive behavior at work leads to altruism, courtesy, extra effort, volunteering for optional tasks, helping others, and being cooperative.[56] An additional study proved that happy employees "are more on-task and waste less time and resources."[57]

Dennis Strigl, former president and COO of Verizon Communications and former CEO of Verizon Wireless, argued that the managers who focus on results are the ones that will have happy employees. The point he is making is that there are four key areas in which employees should focus and achieve results: "growing revenue, getting new customers,

---

53 Ganster, Daniel and Christopher Rosen. "*Work Stress and Employee Health: A Multidisciplinary Review*". Journal of Management 39, no. 5 (2013): 1085-1122.

54 Boehm, Julia and Sonja Lyubomirsky. "*Does Happiness Promote Career Success?*". Journal of Career Assessment 16, no. 1 (2008): 101-116.

55 Ibid.

56 Borman, Walter, Loiuse Penner, Tammy Allen and Stephan Motowidlo. "*Personality Predictors Of Citizenship Performance*". International Journal of Selection and Assessment 9, no. 1-2 (2001): 52-69.

57 Scott, Diane. "*The Managers Role In Increasing Happiness In The Workplace*". Stat Bulletin 78, no. 12 (2009): 11-13.

keeping the customers you already have, and eliminating costs."[58] By focusing on those goals, the level of pride for the work done increases.

The managers who provide the environment for their employees to excel in those areas will be more successful and better perceived by their employees, thus creating a better connection with them and developing a better environment to work in. His argument is that "when results are achieved, pride builds — when pride builds, so does confidence and employees' desire to do better. Good managers understand this."

A *World Economic Forum* report puts it nicely in perspective: "Organizational leaders must be ready and willing to listen to their employees, customers and peers. Though it may seem an easy ask, it requires a broad and enduring commitment. A commitment that not only involves empathy, but also adaptive communication skills and, more importantly, a vision to make it happen, as all organizations, whether digital or analogical, are made up by people."[59]

---

58 Strigl, Dennis. "*Results Drive Happiness: Managers Who Focus On Getting Results From Their Team Will Have Happy Employees*". HR Magazine 56, no. 10 (2011): 113.

59 Beccera, Jorge. "The Digital Revolution Is Not About Technology – It's About People". *World Economic Forum*, Mar. 28, 2017. https://www.weforum.org/agenda/2017/03/the-digital-revolution-is-not-about-technology-it-s-about-people/.

This is really important as we are educating founders on how to treat their early employees and design cultures conducive to productivity. Their success is also the success of the entrepreneurial unit.

* * *

Founders who are more concerned with being liked than getting results tend to excuse under-performance which soon becomes internalized in the culture of the organization. In the short-term, employees appreciate the kindness and flexibility. In the long-term, employees get frustrated and bored with their own lack of drive and performance. Furthermore, the employees who are putting in the extra effort become disinterested in carrying the load.

Personally, I have struggled with this while growing my second start-up. It is a very hard line to draw between being nice and being critically objective. In our case, being full-time college students did not allow us to work a regularly schedueled job forty hours a week, but rather pushed us to work late evening hours,. Sometimes, projects were not completed on time and that hindered our development. After growing a team of twelve over the course of a year-and-a-half, I had to take the hard decision to let some people go and refocus in a smaller, more committed team.

As a start-up, the early employees are like siblings and this is a very difficult relationship to navigate. Support programs have the duty to assist founders through this process and make sure the right dynamic forms among those individuals.

Matt Hartman, partner at Betaworks Ventures, shared in an interview why culture is so important at their office. He describes purposefully crafting a culture of building and making "a culture of geeks," in his own words. Matt acknowledges that they think about this all the time. By allowing their employees to work on side projects just for fun, they are not wasting precious time but rather cultivating curiosity and interest in their workforce plus increasing their ability to create things. Even though many of their people code, the ones who don't are still builders in some ways.

The culture that Betaworks is building doesn't stop at their doorstep. "We are a space even for people who we haven't invested in, nor are co-founders with us, they are still working in our space, building things and regularly come to events to meet each other," Matt shares.

Betaworks' ecosystem has many concentric circles and their core values span across all of them. People can get as involved as they want with the organization, from attending events to building start-ups. It seems to be the culture of the organization that attracts those people in Betaworks' sub-communities, separated in particular categories to group those people interested in a specific area.

CULTURE POINTS / UNITS / STARS / BUCKS

Naturally, as data-driven homo sapiens, we are seeing the link between positive work cultures and productivity and cannot stop but ask ourselves what the return on investment (ROI) is of specific interventions or changes in the organizational design. The question that follows is: can we measure culture?

In a *Wall Street Journal* article, Emily Glazer and Christina Rexrode challenge the concept of company culture as a whole.[60] With officials from the Federal Reserve and other agencies trying to regulate the risky culture of banks on Wall Street, the two authors pose the question of whether the concept of culture itself could be quantified and thus strategically addressed. The companies studied are busy calculating the ratio of happy to grumpy employees or recording the attendance at happy hours. Those measurements of employee behavior seem like nothing more than a disorganized series of anecdotes about the daily lives of bankers, unable to explain the excessive risk-taking occurring.

---

60 Glazer, Emily and Christina Rexrode. "As Regulators Focus on Culture, Wall Street Struggles to Define It". *Wall Street Journal*, Feb. 1, 2015. https://www.wsj.com/articles/as-regulators-focus-on-culture-wall-street-struggles-to-define-it-1422838659.

While some economists might argue that a reduction to a more concrete framework, such as the pattern of accountability that Jensen and Meckling created[61], will provide us with a more concrete plan of attack, psychologists might suggest that people are too complex of an entity to be studied only from one point of view. Thus, it becomes difficult to quantify the culture of an organization, but the effects of it can be blatantly obvious for everyone — both positive and negative.

Can culture go wrong? Absolutely!

In another *Wall Street Journal* article, Rolfe Winkler observes the clear effects of a dysfunctional management team and a broken pattern of accountability in the health-insurance brokerage start-up Zenefits.[62] We are presented with a start-up that resembles more of a fraternity than a company, where abuse of substances is common and even encouraged, specifically after the signing of a big client. Under the corporate motto of "ready, fire, aim," the firm was obsessed with becoming the biggest player in the industry and commonly had long work hours, sometimes more than fifteen per day. This mindset pushed the management to make unethical

---

61 Jensen, Michael and William Meckling. "*Theory of the Firm: Managerial Behavior, Agency Costs and Ownership Structure*". Journal of Financial Economics 3, no. 4 (1976): 305-360.

62 Winkler, Rolfe. "Zenefits Once Told Employees: No Sex in Stairwells". *Wall Street Journal*, Feb. 22, 2016. https://www.wsj.com/articles/zenefits-once-told-employees-no-sex-in-stairwells-1456183097.

decisions, such as cheating on insurance licensing courses in order to speed up the process and not paying employees for unused paid-time off or overtime, thus committing fraud multiple times in California.

If that is not enough, a huge red flag is raised when Parker Conrad, Zenefits founder and original CEO, resigns. At that point in time, we can understand that the company's culture is out of the management's control. The apex of the story comes when Emily Agin, the start-up's director of real estate and workplace services, announces to the firm that the building management company found used condoms in the stairwell and urges the employees to stop having sex on the firm's premises.

Using the Jensen & Meckling framework, one can observe that the flawed evaluation system with rewards based on the quantity and size of the clients, combined with a rather permissive work environment, created both the pressure and the opportunity for such behavior to occur. We can assume that with management's awareness of the problem and lack of intervention, maybe even with their participation, the employees came to rationalize the behavior as normal, thus leading to an unfortunate set of events.

The proposed solutions come in many forms. First, David Sacks the new CEO decided to ban alcohol in the office, trying to ameliorate the effects rather than address the cause of the problems. A simple look in history should inform him that prohibition never came with the intended consequences, especially in a broken system such as Zenefits'. Secondly, Kenneth Baer, Zenefits' spokesperson, announced a plan for the firm to "embrace a new set of corporate values and culture," also missing the point and providing no plan for how that would be achieved.

One of the goals of start-up support units is to prevent cultures like Zenefits' from emerging. It is crucial that the founders are aware of the development of organizational dynamics both during and past the initial stage and proper management systems are put in place. This should entail a careful look on how decision rights are distributed, how the evaluation of employees is conducted, and what rewards are established.

DESIGNING A HEALTHY CULTURE THAT BUILDS HEALTHY CULTURES

Who should take responsibility for all of this work?

It seems to be an easy answer for a small singular program, where the director and their management team can tweak small details as they please. When considering national or even global networks of programs, it is a more difficult question to answer. Should the ecosystem have a consistent feeling? Should they base their development around a specific set of core values and strategy directions? The question might not be whether they *should* but whether they *can*.

When asked about what makes entrepreneurial support units unique, Jess Williamson, former Director of New Accelerators in EMEA and APAC with Techstars, instantly said, "Culture! They take a slightly different personality based on the individuals running the program, no matter how many processes or standard operations you put in place. We are all humans, there is going to be variance among them based on that."

When considering the amount of human interaction that happens in such a program, it is almost impossible to reach a different conclusion. Variables such as how open founders think they can be with the management and how much trust there is between them will greatly influence the dynamics of the organization and the efficiency of the support. It is possible, though, to create a specific set of guidelines that will define the creation of new programs under the same umbrella.

At Techstars, Jess shares that they "focus a lot on being able to listen, ask questions, and allow founders to find answers for themselves." Their manifesto is the Socratic method, which is not pretending that anybody has the answer for anybody else. This type of relationship with founders led them to be very successful across all continents, even when accounting for the unavoidable cultural variance. "When you are pushing boundaries and doing new things, there is a lot of uncertainty and not a one size fits all answer. We try to hire for those types of personality traits especially for the managing director and the program manager. Everybody who interacts with the start-up needs to be "this way"," she shares.

"THE WAY"

So what should we be teaching our entrepreneurs and program managers about empathy when helping them design cultures that will lead to their start-up's / program's success?

First and foremost, give credit where credit is due. This goes a long way in making sure people feel appreciated for their work. It also builds a bridge of trust based on objectivity that empowers people to adopt more ethical work practices.

In meetings, look at everyone in the eyes equally. Sometimes people are less likely to contribute because their physical presence is not acknowledged in the room. On the same topic, make meetings more inclusive by explaining jargon, slang, and history references when those could represent barriers for effective communication. When in doubt about whether you should, it probably is better to explain.

When someone's input is challenged, focus on the context and the idea mentioned instead of shutting down the other person by assuming they are aggressive. Founders who are seeking to be challenged are most likely to succeed because they have the highest chance of receiving that critical feedback and internalizing organizational specific knowledge.

Last but not least, listen instead of just hearing. Everyone has the right to speak and should be treated equally at the table. Successful founders and program managers let everyone finish their ideas without interrupting them. If there is a need for further explanation from the "expert" in the room, make sure that the feedback is constructive rather than providing the chance to patronize the less experienced.

"Being human" is one of the most interesting challenges the globalized, internet-connected 21st century brought us. In the context of supporting entrepreneurship, leading with empathy will result in more successful founders and a more positive work environment for both them and their future employees.

KEY TAKEAWAYS:

- The human aspect of developing support programs will naturally modify the culture of local units even in the context of a national or global initiative. This should be celebrated rather than looked down upon.

- Pushing your founders towards a common goal and acknowledging their success when they get there are good ways to make them happier and more productive.

- Empathy is one of the keys to develop a healthy and positive work culture.

- The culture of a support program will have significant influence on the development of the member start-ups' cultures.

- Success, in the context of a nascent company, can be predicted by the dynamics between the founder / co-founders and the early employees as early signs of corporate culture.

CHAPTER 7

DRIVE, MINDSET & MENTAL HEALTH

———

"Brilliant thinking is rare, but courage is in even shorter supply than genius."

— **PETER THIEL**

"If I quit now, I will soon be back to where I started. And when I started I was desperately wishing to be where I am now."

— **UNKNOWN**

"Don't be afraid to assert yourself, have confidence in your abilities, and don't let the bastards get you down."

— **MICHAEL BLOOMBERG**

Alex Liberman and Austin Rief were helping fellow students at the University of Michigan practice for their interviews when they noticed something that was rather odd. Instead of being driven by a real interest, most students were reading publications such as *Wall Street Journal, Financial Times,* or *The Economist* because they had to. They needed the information to be able to have meaningful and intelligent conversations during their interviews, but did not enjoy the experience at all. The two soon realized that those publications were doing an amazing job at distributing financial information, but not necessarily for our generation. The idea of a business journal for millennials came to mind and would soon become the *Morning Brew.* The question was: How can we teach our generation in a fun and witty way?

In 2015, Alex and Austin started to write as a side-project with the intent of helping other students rather than trying to create a business. The first email sent included their newsletter as a PDF attachment. While initially college-focused, that segment has shrunk to under 30% of their total audience with the average reader now being around 28 years old and working in finance, tech, or consulting. After raising $750,000 in seed funding and not missing delivery on a single day since they started (while also learning what an email service provider is), they were able to grow that project into a profitable start-up with twelve employees and three different newsletters.

How did a student duo who knew nothing about media create a business with over one million daily readers?

In an interview I had with Austin, he shares that it's all about the mindset and willingness to work. "At that point we knew nothing about the media industry, but we were able to fall back on the business knowledge we had." He continues, "I find it very hard to believe that in the era of YouTube, there are people who don't have access to the education required to start a business."

It's the self-starters who succeed since they are able to push themselves to follow their passions and find any means to learn and grow. They are living proof of the "American Dream." Between the people who execute and the idea people, the former will always out-perform the latter. Mark Twain shared that "The secret of getting ahead is getting started. The secret of getting started is breaking your complex over-whelming tasks into smaller manageable tasks, and then starting on the first one."

The job of the supporters becomes encouraging people to actually do something and take the first step. Afterwards, encouraging them to stay level-headed and focused on what their goals are becomes the priority. The *Morning Brew* team took their first hit when, after getting excited about a possible ad deal with the credit card company Discover, the deal fell through. Austin remembers, "In that early stage, the highs are very high, and the lows are very low. You have to continue working." Three months later they were able to restart negotiations and finally sign a deal.

EXECUTION IS KING. PASSION IS ITS QUEEN.

Peter Thiel talks in his book *Zero to One* about how the progress of the world is encouraged by the people who dare to go from zero to one, not from one to many.[63] And that is indeed the hardest step because it requires people to come up with radical solutions to problems and have an absurdly grandiose vision about their ideas and the future. It's the will and courage required to produce that vision which fuels the drive to execute it. The desire to innovate becomes a crucial factor in determining the success of those endeavors and the job of the supporters is to cultivate that desire.

This is indeed difficult for ESUs to do so because people are in different stages of their idea. How do you understand who is serious and who is not?

You sometimes don't, and when you think you do you may be wrong, but nonetheless casting a wider net is better than not casting one at all. Empowering your people to develop

---

63 Thiel, Peter and Blake Masters. *"Zero to One: Notes on Startups, or How to Build the Future"*. Currency, 2014.

this creator mindset and courage is key to building the foundation for other support to follow, no matter how involved those people are at that time.

For support programs and founders alike, the skill is not only differentiating between the ones who are ready and those who are not, but also acting fast when a great prospect comes knocking on the door — whatever shape that door takes. An interesting story comes from a friend of mine Muhammad Miqdad, an incredible entrepreneur and chemical engineer. After aggregating a lot of knowledge about growth strategies across multiple industries, he started analyzing current affairs on his Facebook profile. When he saw that Shayan Sarwar, a fellow Pakistani, won the innovation competition HULT's Dubai round, he added the guy on the platform to congratulate him. Over time, Shayan started appreciating Muhammad's analyses and one day asked him if he would be willing to join him on a trip to China and Japan to find outsourcing partners for his water filtration technology start-up PakVitae. The rest is history, as Muhammad became the business development head soon after.

What drove him was a deep desire to work on large problems and help people. The impact of his work gave him the energy to move past any barriers, including organizational culture miss-alignments. As a U.S.-educated Pakistani working with a team based 11,500 km away, he recalls "a lot of "facepalm" moments happening. Things which seemed obvious to me were alien to my team in Pakistan, and vice versa. It was like grinding two uneven surfaces against each other until they carve each other into two, smooth pieces." When asked if all the struggles were worth it, he answers yes unthinkingly. "What kept me going was the fundamental belief that despite our differences, we were all committed to bringing the best possible solution to the global water crisis to market." Muhammad is now working on his own venture in the same space, partnering with PakVitae to bring clean water to millions of people worldwide.

This teaches us two very important lessons. First, that the drive to succeed has to come from a larger meaning in order to provide the energy to toil day and night on that vision. People who are truly passionate about what they are doing will be fit to embark on a journey to create a start-up. Second, founders like that are hard to find and if hired as employees will soon find ways to break the barriers and go their own route.

It's the responsibility of the programs to not only attract those people but to separate the founder from their idea when making a decision. Just as we saw in the Introduction, Paul Graham made the wise choice to invest in Alexis Ohanian and his business partner, Steve Huffman, even though their first idea wouldn't make the cut.

I wondered if the mindset described holds equally true across cultures. Could it be the case that this drive for entrepreneurship is influenced by other factors?

A study found that among Stanford graduates, children of immigrants, especially Asian Americans, have a higher rate of starting and succeeding at building ventures compared to Americans.[64] It seems to be the case that the act of moving to a new country and starting a new life resembles in approach the act of starting a new business. It involves developing grit and resilience towards failure. This might hold especially true for Asian Americans because, throughout its history, the Chinese society valued stability and harmony above anything else.

Dr. Xiao Wang, the general manager of technology incubator platform InnoSpring Silicon Valley, writes that "with this mindset, in China we've viewed the road to success as getting a university degree and going to work for the government or a large company. The government or company's "innovation" (and many in the US would argue that it's not really

---

64 Lee, Yong Suk and Chuck Eesley. "*The Persistence Of Entrepreneurship And Innovative Immigrants*". Research Policy 47, no. 6 (2018): 1032-1044.

innovation) would be to improve upon already established products or systems."[65]

The Confucian conformity to existing norms is still deeply rooted in people's minds, making the very concept of entrepreneurship different from Western societies. As discussed in the book *China against Herself*, it's hard to blend Schumpeterian entrepreneurship – pioneering new markets and products – with this established notion of order.[66] The very act of breaking apart from that mindset and entering the Western capitalist world of the United States promoted the founding of new businesses.

Cyril Ebersweiler, founder and managing director of the HAX accelerator, shares a funny story from his early days in China: "Starting a business there was a very scary and looked down upon by society thing to do. For my first investment in China, I was on the phone with the parents of the founder, convincing them that their son is working on a real project. After investing a lot in their children, there is this expectation that when older, they will be provided for by them. That leads everyone to be risk averse."

---

65 Wang, Xiao. "U.S. and China Startup Scenes: The Difference". *The Asian Entrepreneur*, Apr. 20, 2016. https://www.asianentrepreneur.org/differences-u-s-china-startup-scenes/.

66 Arayama, Yuko and Panos Mourdoukoutas. "*China Against Herself: Innovation or Imitation in Global Business?*". Praeger, 1999.

GOOD OL' PROCRASTINATION

Motivation varies across entrepreneurs but one thing is certain: we are all humans and we have a natural tendency to procrastinate and delay important tasks. Heidi Grant, a social psychologist and *Harvard Business Review* contributor, describes three reasons people procrastinate:

- Reason #1: You are afraid you will screw it up.

- Reason #2: You don't "feel" like doing it.

- Reason #3: It's hard, boring, or otherwise unpleasant.[67]

If that is the case, it may seem that in order to address the real issue behind procrastination in entrepreneurship we need to understand the underlying causes behind it. Aytekin Tank, founder of JotForm.com, talks about how "as simple as it sounds, identifying the root problem is somewhat contrary to common advice. The internet is filled with articles that advise us to push through feelings of resistance. [...] Productivity hacks are only effective when we know why we're avoiding something in the first place."[68]

---

67   Grant, Heidi. "*How to Make Yourself Work When You Just Don't Want To*". Harvard Business Review, Feb. 14, 2014. https://hbr.org/2014/02/how-to-make-yourself-work-when-you-just-dont-want-to.

68   Tank, Aytekin. "*What I Learned About Procrastination While Scaling My Startup To 4.2 Million Users*". Medium, Nov. 5, 2018. https://medium.com/swlh/what-i-learned-about-procrastination-while-scaling-my-startup-to-4-2-million-users-b07ba29309e.

In an entrepreneurial context, procrastination could be a sign that a founder is working on the wrong thing, but could also be a sign that the founder lacks appropriate guidance. Building a start-up is hectic and sometimes you don't know where to start or what to do. There are days when it feels no progress has been made.

Founders need to embrace uncertainty as a matter of fact.

Those who become immune to the fear of uncertainty are the most well suited to tackle big complex problems. We naturally struggle at understanding ambiguity. Life is not a collection of linear systems; it is a much more complex social system. "Succeeding at building start-ups is as much about serendipity as it is about good intentions and founder ability," stated Hugh Mason, co-founder and CEO of JFDI. Asia shares.

As start-up supporters, it is our duty to educate our founders about this topic and reassure them that the next time they procrastinate, a simple "why?" might be a better solution then their latest BuzzFeed hack.

Are certain entrepreneurs less likely to procrastinate?

When talking about the difference between bootstrapped entrepreneurs and VC-backed ones, Aytekin notes that

"Bootstrappers like myself aren't the only entrepreneurs who sometimes grapple with the snooze button. However, VC-backed founders may have a slight psychological advantage when compared to their bootstrapping counterparts: The pressure that comes with taking someone else's money."

If so far the ideal entrepreneur emerged as the driven, creative, passionate, focused, hard working, innovative, and resilient person, it is my duty to address the other side of the entrepreneurial thinking. The issues come when trying to define procrastination and productivity in a job that doesn't follow any laws of physics but gravitates more towards Jack Ma's 996, where people are encouraged to work 9 am to 9 pm, six days a week.[69]

THE NOT-SO-ROSY PICTURE

It is important to consider both the good and the bad of the entrepreneurial mindset and the pursuit of the "American Dream" in this context. Psychology research in the field of self-determination theory argues that the attainment of goals differs based on the nature of the goal[70] and that this

---

69 Wang, Serenitie and Daniel Shane. "Jack Ma Endorses China's Controversial 12 Hours A Day, 6 Days A Week Work Culture". CNN, Apr. 15, 2019. https://www.cnn.com/2019/04/15/business/jack-ma-996-china/index.html.

70 Kasser, Tim and Richard Ryan. *"Further Examining the American Dream: Differential Correlates of Intrinsic and Extrinsic Goals"*. Personality and Social Psychology Bulletin 22, (1996): 280-287.

difference is mediated by the satisfaction of basic psychological needs — autonomy, competence, and relatedness.[71] While intrinsic goals such as self-acceptance, affiliation, community feeling, and physical health are correlated with increased well-being and less distress, extrinsic goals such as financial success, an appealing appearance, and social recognition are associated with lower vitality and self-actualization.[72] What is essentially being painted is the scientific disapproval of the "American Dream" on which the modern capitalist society rests and the entrepreneurial world prospers.

There seems to be a problem in the way we portray entrepreneurs. The great man theory paints this person with some heroic traits whom nobody believed, but by sticking with it they were able to become successful — to become a "billionaire." This is a great way of telling stories, but nothing more than that. It is not helpful for the few instances where it holds true to portray a false image on the typical entrepreneur. The media does not put enough effort on showcasing the slow systematic growth people usually face because the reality does not drive an audience.

---

71 Niemiec, Christopher, Richard Ryan and Edward Deci. "*The Path Taken: Consequences of Attaining Intrinsic and Extrinsic Aspirations in Post-college Life*". Journal of Research in Personality 43, (2009): 291-306.

72 Kasser, Tim and Richard Ryan. "*Further Examining the American Dream: Differential Correlates of Intrinsic and Extrinsic Goals*". Personality and Social Psychology Bulletin 22, (1996): 280-287.

In a world where developed societies tend to care more and more about how to amass money, we are slowly becoming strangers to our true self. This is one of the reasons we tend to move forward like robots in a race that seems to have no end. Hence, we work harder to get more, we overload our schedules to get more, and we are not satisfied until we achieve "more." The biggest issue is the undefined "more" in the equation that leads to stress, exhaustion, and worse.

Sadly, this has been the trend in our society and its business environment for the last fifty years as studies have shown.[73] There is a constant sprint towards happiness, and many founders confuse it with a rush towards money when they actually miss the whole point of the game. Unfortunately, they are misunderstanding productivity and sacrificing themselves while doing so. As Ladislav Kováč put it, "It seems that achieving zero pain and maximum pleasure has driven the evolution of modern economy."[74] Maybe, instead of focusing on just getting more, we should be re-directing our attention towards living a better, more satisfying life and, as managers and leaders, towards keeping people happy while

---

73   Cabanas, Edgar and José-Carlos Sánchez-González. "*Inverting The Pyramid Of Needs: Positive Psychology's New Order For Labor Success*". Psicothema 28, no. 2 (2016): 107.

74   Kováč, Ladislav. "*The Biology Of Happiness: Chasing Pleasure And Human Destiny*". European Molecular Biology Organization 13, no. 4 (2012): 297-301.

increasing their skills and overall productivity. Can this be achieved in the context of early stage entrepreneurship?

What do Aaron Swartz, co-founder of Reddit and the Creative Commons, Austen Heinz, founder of Cambrian Genomics, Colin Kroll, co-founder of Vine and HQ Trivia, the famous chef-journalist Anthony Bourdain, and actor Robin Williams share in common? Whether it was after or during sitting at the height of success within their industries, they all passed away prematurely. Jake Chapman, in a Techcrunch article, shared that "The most brilliant and creative amongst us are sometimes the most troubled, and nowhere is that clearer than in the entrepreneurial ecosystem."[75] This is the dark side of start-ups that not many speak about. We have explored the drive and the creator mindset as tools necessary for the founders' success but we need to acknowledge that in the race towards building the next unicorn, mental health is often overlooked.

Michael Freeman, along with other researchers from UC Berkeley and Stanford, published a lengthy paper in 2015 describing the state of mental health in entrepreneurship. Their findings were quite shocking. When compared to the average person, founders are:

---

75 Chapman, Jake. "Investors And Entrepreneurs Need To Address The Mental Health Crisis In Startup Culture". *Techcrunch*, Jan. 2019. https://techcrunch.com/2018/12/30/investors-and-entrepreneurs-need-to-address-the-mental-health-crisis-in-startup-culture/.

- two times more likely to suffer from depression

- six times more likely to suffer from ADHD

- three times more likely to suffer from substance abuse

- ten times more likely to suffer from bi-polar disorder

- two times more likely to have psychiatric hospitalization

- two times more likely to have suicidal thoughts[76]

The reality is that start-ups are hard and alienating. Founders are not in a normal day to day job, as they constantly switch hats to complete a variety of tasks. This can and will naturally result in a burnout if one cannot properly delegate. This sense of urgency makes most activities look like an emergency, forcing entrepreneurs to invest more of their energy in the project. Due to the significant time commitment, founders typically spend less time with their loved ones which can make the process feel lonely — even though for most of the time they are in contact with people. Humans need contact outside of their work life in order to feel satisfied.

---

76 Freeman, Michael, Sheri Johnson, Paige Staudenmaier and Macken-zie Zisser. "*Are Entrepreneurs "Touched with Fire"?*". Pre-publication manuscript, 2015.

The long hours do not only pose a threat to the social life of their founders but to their physical health and mental capabilities too. It is not uncommon for entrepreneurs to sleep very few hours, most of those while stressed about the myriad of challenges they are facing. Matt Walker, UC Berkeley professor and researcher, in his famous TED talk presented some of the shocking consequences of sleep deprivation. Research has found that for people who get less than six hours of sleep per night, the hippocampus, which is responsible for encoding new memories into the brain, has significantly reduced activity.[77] Other research from the same lab found that sleep deprivation leads to increased chances of developing numerous neurological and psychiatric disorders.[78]

Add this to the incredible responsibility founders have, both financially and emotionally, and you have the perfect recipe for a disaster. Entrepreneurs need to develop a thick skin to succeed, but the pressure that comes along can break people from within.

In the previously mentioned article, Jake Chapman writes "Addressing the ongoing mental health catastrophe in

---

77 Abel, Ted, Robbert Havekes, Jared Saletin and Matthew Walker, "*Sleep, Plasticity and Memory from Molecules to Whole-Brain Networks*". Current Biology 23, no. 17 (2013): R774-R788.

78 Krause, Adam, Eti Ben Simon, Bryce Mander, Stephanie Greer, Jared Saletin, Andrea Goldstein-Piekarski and Matthew Walker. "*The Sleep-deprived Human Brain*". Nature Reviews Neuroscience 18, no. 7 (2017): 404+.

entrepreneurship is a moral imperative, and for wise investors, it should be a function of doing business. Venture capitalists make their living off the blood, sweat and tears of founders. It is through their passion and efforts that we succeed or fail. We can either choose to see founders purely as a means to an end (generating returns) or we can see them as the whole people they are."[79]

WHERE DO WE START?

With self-care or a work-life balance mostly nonexistent in the life of the founder, it becomes the responsibility of the ecosystem one is involved in to provide the required support and guidance while navigating this journey. We see over and over again how entrepreneurs are paying themselves last or taking the least vacation of all employees, and we normalize this behavior not just by allowing it to happen but by celebrating its occurrence. This is one of the true tragedies of the entrepreneurial world.

What can be done to address this?

First and foremost, fighting the stigma against mental health in entrepreneurship requires open dialogue between founders and their supporters, both investors and program

---

79 Chapman, Jake. "Investors And Entrepreneurs Need To Address The Mental Health Crisis In Startup Culture". *Techcrunch*, Jan. 2019. https://techcrunch.com/2018/12/30/investors-and-entrepreneurs-need-to-address-the-mental-health-crisis-in-startup-culture/.

managers. It has to be appropriate for people to be vulnerable with each other and seek out help when needed. This builds a foundation for mutual trust to develop and will greatly enhance not just the relationship among the mentioned individuals but also increase the effectiveness of the other resources offered by the program.

On a more concrete note, investing in specific resources for founders would ensure that investors stay true to their mission of supporting entrepreneurs. In the words of Jake Chapman, "the participants in this ecosystem, need to put our money where our mouths are when we say that we are "founder-friendly" and "invest in founders first.."" [80] Take the example of DMZ, a tech start-up accelerator in Toronto, Canada, which included mental health as one of their top priorities and partnered with an online counseling platform to provide their network, consisting of over four hundred people, with access to free therapy. Abdullah Snobar, the executive director, shares that "it's not about solving the fact that individuals will come to face high levels of stress and anxiety. It's about finding ways to equip them with the proper tools to maneuver the daily ups and downs of start-up life." [81] The ROI of such resources goes well past what money can measure.

---

80 Ibid.
81 Snobar, Abdullah. "Getting Honest About Mental Health In The World Of Tech Startups". *Forbes*, Aug. 8, 2018. https://www.forbes.com/sites/forbestechcouncil/2018/08/08/getting-honest-about-mental-health-in-the-world-of-tech-startups/#65c91903641a.

Erin Frey, co-founder of Hellokip, provides a great analogy to understand the size of the investment one can make in providing those services: "Therapy in the Bay Area costs roughly $200/session. If a founder goes a few times a month, that's a small investment to ensure a high-performing leadership team. Put another way, a founder could spend the equivalent amount of money per year on a top of the line Macbook plus related accessories. What's more valuable to a company – a high performing founder or a high performing laptop?."[82] When put into perspective, it doesn't seem too much anymore, does it?

As we discussed in Chapter 6, the culture of the support program will naturally flow in the culture of the member start-ups. When crafted properly, it should allow everyone in the ecosystem to be vigilant of each other, recognize when people are under too much stress and react by asking for help, either for them or for others. A healthy and friendly community will enable its participants to reach their full potential and reduce the risk of severe events occurring.

---

82 Frey, Erin. "The Investor Pledge for Mental Health". *Medium*, May 30, 2017. https://medium.com/kip-blog/the-investor-pledge-for-mental-health-a59edef02076.

KEY TAKEAWAYS:

- Patience and consistency are values that need to sit at the core of entrepreneurial education endeavors of support programs.

- The determination of the founders is one of the key factors predicting the chance of success among start-ups.

- Execution is king.

- Procrastination among founders could be a sign of lack of proper guidance and support.

- The "American Dream" could be a double edged sword.

- Mental health should be a top priority for support units looking to have healthy founders. Specific programming is necessary to address the issues entrepreneurs are facing.

- Founders are at very high risk for psychiatric and psychological illness, compared to most other professions. This needs the attention of all stakeholders in the ecosystem.

CHAPTER 8

ASSUMPTIONS, ITERATIONS & PIVOTS

———

"Your assumptions are your windows on the world. Scrub them off every once in a while, or the light won't come in."

- *ISAAC ASIMOV*

"If we tried to think of a good idea, we wouldn't have been able to think of a good idea. You just have to find the solution for a problem in your own life."

- *BRIAN CHESKY*

"Pivoting is not the end of the disruption process, but the beginning of the next leg of your journey."

- *JAY SAMIT*

When asked to share some of the most revealing moments in the start-up he helped, entrepreneur and venture capitalist Dan Khan recalls how "some of the companies I worked with were so sure they were onto something, so certain that there is a market for their product, so stuck in their assumptions, that they were unable to pivot."

How stuck?

A group of people were working on a start-up that was scanning horses feet with a camera in order to design horseshoes that were later 3D printed and delivered to the customers. It all sounded like, and probably was a great idea and the team spent a lot of time developing a prototype and the software. After all, why not take advantage of the latest technologies to replace old processes such as horseshoe manufacturing? The only caveat is that the team got carried away with their product development without speaking to their target customers -- no farriers (the craftsmen trimming and shoeing the horses), no horse owners, nothing. I'm still trying to figure out who wakes up one day thinking about scanning horse feet and 3D printing horseshoes for them. The team decided to join an accelerator and during their time there, the pressure was high. They spent countless hours and lots of money on developing something that was based mostly on non-validated assumptions. Dan Khan suggested them talking with potential customers which they did.

The problem? No one was willing to buy their product.

Everyone enjoyed the cool idea and concept, but no one found it useful nor wanted to use it. More and more customer discovery interviews and the same responses kept on piling up. Halfway through the accelerator, they gave in and realized there was no market for their product.

The problem most people face when building new businesses is that they are not engaging with the industry and the people they are creating for. This external view of how they think the market works is based on assumptions, not evidence, and can be misleading. The successful entrepreneurs are able to empathize with their audience and define their problems and pain points. They constantly expose themselves to the industry and experience what the market is experiencing. The moral of the story is to make sure you are actually solving a problem before you are spending resources on the solution.

This story though is not one with a sad ending. The team was able to pivot completely and move to a new idea. This time rooted in genuine customer insights. In 2014, they started working on what is now known as mish.guru and they were able to build a radically new company in just two years after realizing their initial idea wouldn't work.

So what was the new idea?

A software-first storytelling agency, selling Snapchat and Instagram story marketing services for big brands including Visa, McDonald's, Vodafone, and Bank of Ireland. They since moved from the beautiful land of New Zealand to Brooklyn, New York and generated over one million dollars in revenue. Sometimes, all you need is a kick in the back to remind you not to take your assumptions for granted.

* * *

Noel Joyce has been at HAX since the very beginning of the accelerator, now the head of design. His mission is to help founders develop the best version of the product. "They need to define why they did things and why they didn't do other things; if they can't answer that, they haven't really explored anything," he says. By providing the founders with a set of tools that allows them to replicate the process of design, Noel and the team at HAX are building sustainable businesses, not just start-ups. They are able to mitigate the planning fallacy and get founders to think deeply about what they are creating.

Noel shares that "If you get a good team of entrepreneurs, they are willing to listen to the advice of both the support team and their customers too. They need to understand that the first product is the entry point in their entrepreneurial journey, not the end. This is how we are de-risking our investments through design."

Take the example of Nomiku, a HAX-accelerated manufacturing start-up, building sous vide devices for people to use at home. Initially, it was a large device that was funky to use. "When I saw the prototype I was like 'oh, this might not work, we'll need to iterate," Noel recalls. Given the size of the pot, one could expect less usage and more time in storage. It just didn't make sense. Furthermore, sous vide was not a big thing anyway for people other than high end chefs. The question for Nomiku and the HAX team was "How do you on-board people on this new technology?."

After several iterations, they came up with a device that clips on a normal cooking pot that customer probably already had and were familiar with. A redesigned interface that resembled a faucet was easy to use and made people not feel stupid when looking at the device. Needless to say, the product was a success. Nowadays, most sous vide devices are using the same design specs as Nomiku. "We created the industry standard for sous vide cooking" says Noel.

PERSPECTIVES = $$$

Doug Chambers and Julian Clayton were born and raised in construction, having the industry running through their veins. The latter first swung a hammer for a paycheck at the young age of twelve. While they lived it and breathed it, key difference: Julian never built anything taller than two stories, where Doug was in the skyscrapers business. In Doug's world, you design and execute five to six projects before you retire, while in Julian's you might complete forty to fifty in one year. The two ended up collaborating on Fieldlens, a construction-tech start-up that was later acquired by the co-working giant WeWork.

Their recipe for success: never basing Fieldlens' strategic decision on only one point of view. Individually they could easily be wrong, but together it's way harder to be so.

There has to be a collaboration between clashing school of thoughts in order to design products fit for a larger portion of an industry or a market. Sir Jonathan Ive, the famous designer at Apple, shared why teamwork is an important part of this process. "One of the things that is particularly precious about working at Apple is that many of us on the design team have worked together for 15-plus years and there's a wonderful thing about learning as a group. A fundamental part of that is making mistakes together. There's no learning without trying lots of ideas and failing lots of times."[83]

And it's the responsibility of the individuals to become more aware, educate themselves and understand the perspectives

83   Richmond, Shane. "Jonathan Ive Interview: Simplicity Isn't Simple". *The Telegraph*, May 23, 2012. https://www.telegraph.co.uk/technology/apple/9283706/Jonathan-Ive-interview-simplicity-isnt-simple.html.

that they are bringing to the table, since no one else will be creating products for them. Collaboration and debate will be the only way progress will be made. That's how bad ideas get weeded out. People have to come to terms with the reality of the situation: sometimes their idea sucks or it is just not different enough and mimics something that already exists in the market. Julian Clayton mentions that there is this misconception that "just because someone hand an idea and was charismatic enough to raise capital to fund it, they are automatically right." And so many people fall in that trap. During our interview, he recalled a great story to back this up:

"There is this restaurant in his town that is changing hands every eight months and owner after owner they all keep making the same mistake and fail over and over again. We are talking about an establishment housed in a prime real estate building, downtown with incredible amounts of foot traffic going past the door every day. And somehow, every new owner decides to open a "new" bar & grill when truly there is nothing new to it. Around it? Countless specialized restaurants with great building designs and a real personality. Three blocks away in any direction, countless other bar & grills. No matter how many people failed, no one seemed to figure out why there is no market pull for the innovative bar & grill in the area. But year after year, John's, Bob's, Frank's, Jim's, you name it keeps popping out in the same space."

* * *

Lots of people believe they have a great idea, without putting any effort into even researching if it has been done before. There should be no attention paid to those people who haven't spoken to a single customer before patting themselves on the back for their amazing inspiration. It might be that their idea was already built two years ago. They have not admitted to themselves that they have no differentiator to bring to the market. And when there is no differentiation, making people pay you for the service or product becomes an almost impossible task — "it's hard to make people give you a dollar these days," Julian mentions. You have to be developing something that can connect with the people you are creating for, and invite them to step through your door be it physical or digital. This cannot be done from the comfort of your corner office.

The importance of assumption testing should not be ignored as it is only with constant customer feedback that we can create products truly fit for a market. The job of entrepreneurial support units is to make sure their start-ups are diligent in their customer discovery process and push their founders to think twice about what they think is right and will work. The truth is that most of the time we do not know what is right or wrong. Since innovation is the process of going through with an idea all the way to its fruition, we can infer that most of that work comes from implementation rather than invention.

Paul Graham shares in one of his essays that "When experts are wrong, it's often because they're experts on an earlier version of the world."[84] The world is not static and people have to have an undying belief in the concept of change. After all, Heraclitus the Greek philosopher has been quoted as saying "change is the only constant in life."

Mark Wilson, University of Rochester professor and co-founder of the Pre-Seed Workshop—one of the world's earliest "pre-accelerator" bootcamps dedicated to hard-science startups, says that this realization "takes us away from the Eureka moment mindset and brings us to the reality: 99% of all innovation is incremental ideas, very little is a radical breakthrough." He goes on to describe what he coined as "innovation creed". Before getting into any details about any ideas, this largely-missing part of entrepreneurial support and education asks why a founder is doing what they are doing and how are they going to measure success. The drivers behind why people do the things they do helps us analyze the biases they are bringing to the table, what "kinds" of ideas are right for them, and which pathways forward are most appropriate. His personas include the Wannabe Tycoon, the

---

84 Graham, Paul. "How to Be an Expert in a Changing World" *Essays of Paul Graham*, Dec. 2014. http://www.paulgraham.com/ecw.html.

Simple Proprietor, the Hopeless Humanitarian, the Perpetual Hobbyist, the Mad Scientist, the Flipper, the Lucky Licensor, and the Panicked Executive.

Many programs rush out to help everyone along a "Wannabe Tycoon" pathway when this is quite in conflict with the priorities and actions for someone wanting to be a "Simple Proprietor". The reason behind why people do the things they do helps us analyze the biases they are bringing to the table. Programs need to aid founders in assessing the "why" early on in the innovation process to make sure the major drivers are understood.

* * *

Dan Khan is no superhero, but his first entrepreneurial endeavor might portray him as one. He has been working in start-ups since 1998, right after he graduated from college. His first job was in a tech start-up that was very successful in building a social network in the U.K. during the early Dot-Com Boom. They reached a couple million users in a short period of time, and as things were going great they decided to sell. Luck and fortune made it that their exit was at the height of the boom, right before the dot com bubble burst, sending most tech companies into a downward spiral. This is an unusual start for an entrepreneur, who usually builds on top of their failures before reaching success.

But that shouldn't mislead you into thinking Dan's career was marked only by successes. He happens to have had many failures in his life or as he calls them, "naive things you learn down the line." Right after the social network success, he went on to try to sell luxury sports cars online through a prize competition. You probably remember the last time you were in an airport or a shopping mall and you saw luxury cars sitting on fancy pedestals with a ribbon on the hood. The car you have been dreaming since you were a child, now in front of you as you are ready to go on your well-deserved holiday or right in the middle of your shopping spree. The catch? Some sort of highly priced ticket or offer that could get you a chance of leaving home with the big prize.

So why not replicate the same model on this cool new thing: the internet. Armed with the experience and confidence of having already built a successful product on this new platform, Dan and his team tried to adapt the same business model in the U.K., but purely online. They spent over a year building the website and the system, and as an yet inexperienced founder, he left all the customer discovery to the side.

The early days seemed promising, giving them enough traction to think that they were onto something. Soon after though, the growth stalled and couldn't move any further. They have reached their peak. But how can a company reach its peak so early into the game? Well, sometimes the pie is just not as big as you anticipated.

They failed to realize that car brands and dealerships had exclusive deals with airports and shopping malls that offered them multiple benefits for keeping only their cars in those spaces. And why does the physical space matter so much? It really doesn't. It's *why* the customer is in that space that matters the most. It's the moment of relaxation that people experience when they are not thinking about work because they are ready to embark on a flight to their dream destination or spend the next couple hours roaming through shops trying on and buying different things. All of that didn't happen online, not when they were on the website.

Another missed aspect was the physicality of the experience. What initially captures the audience is not thinking that they might own that car one day. They are first looking at the car, touching it, getting excited imagining themselves behind the steering wheel. Only now are they dreaming about fulfilling their childhood desires and taking it home. It's very hard for a website to compete with that moment of joy. Pictures of cars are never as good as the car itself.

There was a critical error made on the business model, which is that the customer desire wouldn't fluctuate between the two different environments. They didn't lose on customer need, they lost on the competitive advantage because their slice of the pie was too small to feed the growth of the start-up. They simply couldn't compete with the physical locations offering the same solution. It went deeper than technical issues, it was one of the core assumptions of the business that was slowly failing. Dan and his team failed to realize that in the premature stages of the start-up. "We misjudged what made the market tick and why people buy, so ultimately we had some big leap of faith assumptions that we hadn't uncovered and that led to the business not working" he shares.

Entrepreneurs tend to not perform enough due diligence when they fall in love with the solution. They fail to question their assumptions, especially when dealing with the luxury market because there is some social status that goes along with it. It becomes great party conversation to say you're in the luxury industry and thus people want to associate.

Unfortunately, this leaves room for error and young innovators can easily fall into that trap. They are not alone, investors also start buying into the story without considering the core of the business and thus the vicious behavior is perpetuated until someone realizes the mistake. For Dan and his team, this project was dead, but boy did they learn something from it.

* * *

It is not always assumptions about the business model that can kill a project, but sometimes is the assumptions about the technology that prevent an idea from succeeding. Ben Gilbert, co-founder of not one but two start-up studios, Madrona Venture Labs and Pioneer Square Labs, shared a great story to back this point up. At PSL, they try to do one or two projects that are really out there in terms of technical risk. One of their ideas came after one of the employees read a paper about a new means of accessing RAM that a software wouldn't normally have access to and make the bits flip. They thought they could build and market a system where a piece of software would be running on machines and measure how many bits flip in an attempt to analyze radiation levels in the surroundings.

They went ahead and hired a well-known PhD researcher to work on this problem with them and figured out that they were right, high levels of radiation would make those bits flip, but so would small variations in temperature. They had built a software that was able to recognize mostly nothing and provide very little value to the end consumer. This story has a happy ending though: the researcher ended up staying with the studio which granted them one of the world's best experts in machine learning. This allowed them to spin out three machine learning start-ups that performed very well because they got access to incredible talent at an early stage.

There seems to be this inflexibility and rigidity of thought in terms of product development that characterizes entrepreneurs who fail at innovation. It's easy to dream about all the cool and amazing things we could be doing, but way harder to take the time and energy to put those things to the test and allow change to happen. The rule seems simple: "If the final product you end up developing is the exact same as your original idea, you are wrong." Successful product development is characterized by constant iteration due to the convergence of different perspectives. We are required to constantly capture information from the market in order to challenge our ways of thinking because we might, as is often the case, be wrong.

* * *

So far, we have seen that assumptions make or break a start-up idea and should be analyzed very seriously. The question that naturally follows is how do we go about thinking and analyzing those things? I would argue that the process might be easier than one would expect. It all starts with a shift in mindset by understanding that we all bring biases to the table, and unless we spend some time to analyze our own decision things could go bad very fast.

Tools such as the Business Model Canvas and the Value Proposition Canvas allowed innovators and entrepreneurs to test their assumptions early and created an industry shift towards an efficient customer discovery process. At the Barbara J. Burger iZone, I use those tools with my clients early-on in the consulting project in order to get an understanding of what sets the foundation for the potential start-up to happen. Every single time, they have revealed assumptions that the client never thought about and helped with adjusting accordingly.

We have to understand that those tools were not always available, and for a long time, business people failed to properly test their hypothesis and biases before going on and building products and services. Seasoned marketer and product manager recently turned professor John Schloff recalls a moment when his team failed to deliver on the promises, quoting the lack of the tools he is now teaching about as an important factor of their failure.

He was working for an organization with a large base of small and medium business customers. Having already built stable relationships and a steady cash flow, John challenged his team to brainstorm some other opportunities to get extra dollars. They started looking at the commonalities between their customers and since the majority were small and medium business, they all had a passion for branded hats, t-shirts, mouse pads, coffee mugs, you name it. Everything that had their logo on it was at one point sitting on someone's desk. Their company itself had a great relationship with an organization doing custom materials for them, so, counting on their great brand and stable customer base, an idea popped out: What if they could take those materials and distribute them through their own channel? Revenues looked good in the industry, the execution seemed reasonably easy, so there was little reason to say no to a new business opportunity.

The thing they never actually questioned was if it made sense for a company in their industry to tackle the issue of custom branded materials. The only tests done were on the execution of an idea never validated. Yes, it was possible to do it, but that didn't provide any insight on the question "should we do it?." John says that having had tools like the Business Model Canvas or the Value Proposition Canvas, they would have been "culturally forced to identify those assumptions" and thus empowered to test them.

He believes they would have surely changed the idea and not wasted so much time and energy on a product that didn't matter. Maybe even some alternative approaches would have been discovered. The project ended up being worked on for a long time without finding any success. It never formally became an integrated part of the company, basically never leaving the incubation phase. A costly mistake for a set of untested assumptions. All that was needed was a drive to explore their basic underlying hypothesis.

KEY TAKEAWAYS:

- Assumption testing has to be done continuously throughout the innovation process but should be started as early and as cheaply as possible.

- A founder that did not talk with any potential customer is not a founder, but a dreamer. No investment should follow.

- Assumptions come in many forms: about the customer, about the business model, about the technology, about the industry, and more. All of them should be tested.

- Nowadays, there are tools to make assumption testing accessible to all entrepreneurs. Strategyzer's Business Model Canvas and Value Proposition Canvas are great places to begin.

- If a business doesn't pivot and follow the needs of the market, it will become irrelevant and go bankrupt.

PART III

THE THEORY
IN ACTION

CHAPTER 9

DEVELOPING ENTREPRENEURIAL COMMUNITIES

"Never doubt that a small group of thoughtful, committed people can change the world. Indeed, it is the only thing that ever has."

— MARGARET MEAD

"If you want to go quickly, go alone. If you want to go far, go together."

– AFRICAN PROVERB

"I'm from Michigan originally. I came to Seattle for the first time after graduating from college with a degree in computer science to interview at some tech companies in the area and fell in love with the city. It is truly beautiful and has something special to it that just gave me a feeling that it was the place to be. Even if I didn't get the job I wanted, I was able to find a position to volunteer in middle school computer lab three hours away from the city. I remember how in the weekends some friends and I would jump in the car to see shows in the city and come back at 4-5 in the morning. There was a vibe to the city that made it appealing to us and I never left. The tech scene here is very interesting too. I soon found a job at Microsoft and during that time I started attending some start-up meetups in the basement of a small library. It was 20 of us and we would share ideas and projects that we were working on and get beers afterwards. At the same time, a lot of Start-up Weekends started happening around town and at one of them I found my co-founder. Those programs were the catalyst for me to become an entrepreneur." This is what Kevin Leneway, co-founder and CTO of Haiku Deck, an AI-powered presentation builder that raised over $5 million in funding and is being used by millions of people worldwide, shared during our interview.

I began wondering if there is something special about that story that could direct my research. What was unique about Kevin's journey that led him building one of the most popular iPad apps of all time? More precisely, what was unique about the city he was in when working on that idea?

As we look around the world, we see a large concentration of start-up activity around cities that are now known as global innovation clusters such as San Francisco, Toronto, New York City, London, Tel Aviv, Tokio, Beijing, Shanghai, and Shenzhen. Apart from those top tier start-up destinations, a close second bracket of innovative cities such as Los Angeles, Singapore, Boston, Paris, Seattle, Austin, Seoul, and Berlin follows. Buried in God-knows where are the emerging start-up communities of Pittsburgh, Salt Lake City, Omaha, Cincinnati, and many others around the world. I questioned whether what built the former is now building the latter or the new wave of start-up hotspots fuels at a different gas station.

In a conversation with Ben Elowitz, managing director at Madrona Venture Labs (MVL), he talks about building a successful start-up studio by pairing "A+ ideas with A+ talent": "where you have enough talent and expertise to create something strong, that's where entrepreneurial activity flourishes." This is one of the reasons MVL strategically focuses on machine learning and artificial intelligence since Seattle has such a strong pool of talent in those verticals. Even when this is the case, Ben shares that the city's "robust talent market is underserved by venture capital, and would-be entrepreneurs do not have enough connections who are angel investors, founders, or VCs." The community is not the founding ground of the entrepreneurial activity but rather the catalyst for its growth. What large clusters like New York City, San Francisco, or London did was to evolve channels for connections and partnerships to happen.

WHO SHOULD TAKE THE LEAD?

On the surface level, the debate stands between the public and the private sector. When analyzing both in detail, one can observe that both are such complex entities that even if we were to pick one we wouldn't reach a conclusion. Suppose the answer is the private sector. Who is the private sector? Is it the VCs, the founders themselves, helpful angel investors, or is it the accelerators, incubators, and consulting companies?

In East Asia, with China in particular, we see a heavy influence of the public sector in leading entrepreneurial initiatives. A *South China Morning Post* article reports that "the central government has launched more than 1,600 high-tech incubators across China, and more than 20 per cent of the country's National Social Security Fund has been allocated to venture capital and private equity investments."[85]

---

85 Jing, Meng and Amanda Lee. "Where is China's Silicon Valley?". South China Morning Post, Aug. 12, 2017. https://www.scmp.com/tech/start-ups/article/2106494/where-chinas-silicon-valley.

On the other side of the Pacific, the private sector has long been fueling the growth of entrepreneurial activity. With the positive results now in full light, local and national administrations are starting to not just pay closer attention but to get involved in aiding those initiatives. Across the board we can see increased efforts to support incubators and accelerators, make seed funding more available, reduce licensing hurdles, provide access to networks of experienced mentors, and build partnerships with local universities.

In a *Techcrunch* article, Representative Steve Chabot shared that the administration should focus on "removing barriers to capital and supporting new innovative models of funding, such as peer-to-peer lending and equity-based crowdfunding. It also requires a flexible, light-touch regulatory environment that embraces disruptive technologies. Finally, we must rethink how we utilize public resources. More emphasis should be placed on helping the underserved learn entrepreneurial skills, because these are the building blocks that will create more opportunities."[86]

It has been seen in research that entrepreneurial ecosystems are a key element of the successful development of national entrepreneurial initiatives as they are able to creatively bring

---

86 Chabot, Steve. "The Rise of Entrepreneurial Communities". *Techcrunch*, 2015. https://techcrunch.com/2015/10/03/the-rise-of-entrepreneurial-communities/.

together previously separated resources and make them available in a more collaborative way.[87] The path towards developing sustainable entrepreneurial ecosystems requires the participation of all stakeholders, both private and public.

But what happens when those partnerships don't work out? Could foreign initiatives mediate that?

* * *

Mike Lightman is anything but a boring person. He has been in the Peace Corps serving in Morocco, where he ran several entrepreneurial projects. He cold called his way to a venture capital job after his MBA and mentored start-ups at some of the world's largest accelerators and incubators such as HAX, Urban-X, 1776, and SXSW. He is now a managing partner at New York City-based venture firm, Big Idea Ventures.

One of the most interesting stories he has comes from his work with the World Bank where he was building start-up ecosystems around the globe. His first assignment was to work with was a clean technology focused incubator in Jamaica called the Caribbean Climate Innovation Center, which at that point was not working very well.

---

87   Drexler, Alejandro, Greg Fischer, and Antoinette Schoar. *"Keeping It Simple: Financial Literacy and Rules of Thumb"*. American Economic Journal: Applied Economics 6, no. 2 (2014): 1-31.

The way the World Bank partners with local agencies is by putting out a request for proposals on entrepreneurial support programs. So the group that had won that particular bid was a partnership between a government-backed Jamaican research group and a public-private group from Trinidad and Tobago.

After a year, the World Bank realized that all they have done is giving out about half a million dollars to about ten or eleven companies and precisely nothing else — no additional support, no follow up investment, no check on how the money was spent. The recipients of funding ranged from existing and operational companies to crazy ideas on a piece of paper with no execution.

That is where Mike comes in. "We need you to go in, kickoff several bootcamps and an accelerator in the next six to eight months or we're gonna lose our funding. Also, make it in a way that is replicable to other countries in the Caribbean ecosystem," he was told. Easy task, right?

He came up with a strategy that involved a four-phase program where they do pilots in Jamaica and Trinidad and then they replicate the program with a hub and spoke model across the Caribbean, have a "Start-"p Weekend" type of event to help them ideate and brainstorm and then transition them to an early stage accelerator to help them actually build that first product and sell it to their first customer. Partners such the water authority, the power authority, and other NGOs were brought in to talk about the biggest issues they deal with and the kind of solutions they need to see.

"And... the whole thing was a disaster," Mike shares.

The reasons behind it are complex, but two that stand out are culture and decision-making authority. Culturally, the Caribbean is very different than the United States -- and there is a guy from New York City who comes in and tells people how they're going to do their job. It doesn't always work.

The bigger problem was the Jamaican government and the Trinidadian government. "They kept saying 'No, no, no, the culture in our country is different. We do things differently here!' and kept things strictly cultural missing the whole point of the initiative," says Mike. "At the opening ceremony of the accelerators there was no mention of the start-ups involved! It was a series of ministers patting each other on the back about how great they are for doing this, some traditional dances, hors d'oeuvres and cocktails. That's it! I was the only person that went and spoke with the entrepreneurs."

If you want to make a change, you need to have decision power or at least influence. Just giving other people advice on what to do and acting as a consultant is exceedingly difficult in this environment, because the reason that they didn't want to change wasn't the lack of great ideas, but the lack of execution. The World Bank literally came in as advisers having no authority in the area.

It was and will always be at the latitude of the people who are there to decide where they are heading. After all, it's their community. You must have the support of all local stakeholders on a vision level in order to drive meaningful change. One should expect, in introducing entrepreneurial support units in new communities, the same kind of adoption curve you see for new products and services in the market.

What else builds those successful organic ecosystems? What drives those communities together?

IT MIGHT TAKE MORE THAN A HAMMER AND NAILS TO BUILD IT

Jeff Slobotski is not your average entrepreneur, but one committed to developing entrepreneurial communities wherever he is. Jeff served on the board of the Greater Omaha Chamber of Commerce and is a member of the World Economic Forum's "Young Global Shapers". Tony Hsieh, the famous founder and CEO of Zappos, once said that "the way that Jeff and his team are putting the Midwest on the map has been inspiring. He is gifted at building authentic relationships to both connect and amplify the energy that's taking place within the region and beyond."[88]

So I went and talked with him about how to empower communities to become more entrepreneurial and how to best support local entrepreneurs on their quest for recognition and fame. He recalls experiencing the entrepreneurial ecosystems of San Francisco, New York, Boulder, and Boston while he was working at a technology company in 2008 and being amazed by the drive and inspiration of the people there. They "push forward with new ideas and launch new business every day," he said. Returning home to Omaha, Nebraska, he was upset to see equally well-equipped people working alone and being unaware of the innovation that was happening around them.

There was a lack of information shared among the local innovators and that's when he decided to found Silicon Prairie News, a website aimed to highlight the amazing creatives in their own backyard. He mentions that his goal was never to build the next Silicon Valley, but rather to "take the strengths and assets that are unique to our region, and build upon

---

88   From Jeff's personal website. https://www.jeffslobotski.com/.

them." His new goal: to increase the connections between the countless innovators in the Midwest.

Four years after starting his mission, he shared the three key components that are vital to generate an entrepreneurial region in an article in the *Times Magazine*[89]. His three elements were:

- growing the community

- highlighting and sharing the work of others

- getting people together through events and gatherings

It is important that every community has a champion, or a group of individuals who are passionate about the development of the area. The process will take time, so you need people focused on the macro picture and are able to put the effort for the long-haul. Commitment to and belief in the evolution of the ecosystem is key to this part. The goal is to empower people to get involved in the process, which won't happen overnight.

89 Slobotski, Jeff. "First There Was Silicon Valley. Then Silicon Alley. Now...the Case for Building Silicon Prairie". *Time Magazine*, Jun. 19, 2012. http://business.time.com/2012/06/19/first-there-was-silicon-valley-then-silicon-alley-now-the-case-for-building-silicon-prairie/.

The second key aspect is to build an information system to get those people in the spotlight and highlight their work and success. The medium itself is not that important as long as the residents can be updated on the innovative work that is being done in their own backyard. While working at Silicon Prairie News, he recalls having *Inc. Magazine* reach out to them one day in 2007 asking about the companies they should be paying attention to. The question was "who should we follow?" Easy task for a group of people whose main job was to keep track of the innovators in their area.

The company they selected was Hudl, a software company on a mission to revolutionize the way coaches and athletes prepare for and stay ahead of the competition. Founded by David Graff, Brian Kaiser, and John Wirtz in 2006 in Lincoln, Nebraska, Hudl now offers the tools to edit and share videos, interact with statistics, and create quality highlight reels for entertainment and recruiting purposes. The whole experience is available online, giving coaches and athletes secure access at home and while traveling. At that point, they were a small start-up with sixteen to twenty employees and a great vision. Fast forward twelve years and you will see a company with 1,100 employees around the globe that closed a $72.5 million funding round led by Accel in 2015, and has 4.3 million unique users on its platform. Hudl was named one of the most innovative companies by *FastCompany*.

Jeff and his team were trying to highlight and raise the visibility of some great companies in the area, and little did they know that the small backyard start-up would grow into such a powerful entity. Their goal is to tell stories, and tell them loudly. Although he acknowledges that their intro to *Inc. Magazine* was not the key driver of Hudl's success, it is important to note the help they provided. All of that is possible when you have people actively engaged in monitoring the progress of start-ups.

The third important aspect is physically bringing people together. He recalls meeting author Sarah Lacy in Omaha while she was on tour for her first book, *Once You're Lucky, Twice You're Good,* and even if only one hundred twenty people showed up, it was the first time entrepreneurs, investors, professors, and others were sitting next to each-other in a dedicated event. That was the stepping stone for Jeff's large ambitions, empowering him to start working on what is now known as Big Omaha. The event year- after- year brings hundreds of innovators to listen to people such as Gary Vaynerchuck, Jonathan Badeen, Amy Emmerich, and Elizabeth Gore. The benefit is two-sided; local talent gets exposure and interacts with national innovators and investors, while the latter gets a new understanding of the Midwest entrepreneurial opportunities.

Jeff says that "building entrepreneurial communities is a long-term play full of incremental changes in the short term." It is important to keep the big goal in mind while you put years of work into making things happen. I believe any region has the potential to become a great hub for innovation, as long as there are people living in it. The example of Omaha and Jeff's great work in the Midwest should serve as a reminder that creative individuals can be found anywhere, and potential just has to be discovered and their story shared. Afterwards, the goal is to accelerate the connection between those entrepreneurs, local capital, mentors, and key stakeholders. This seems to be the case in more places than just Nebraska.

750 MILES WEST

While in the early 2000s, venture capital was hard to find in the state of Utah, nowadays we can see a booming technology scene with significant deals every year. The scarce access to capital enabled companies such as Qualtrics and Pluralsight to achieve world class operational efficiency that fueled growth. In fact, these companies were bootstrapped for years before raising significant venture capital for the first time in the early 2010s. The graph below shows just how much the Beehive State's entrepreneurial scene grew in the past decade.

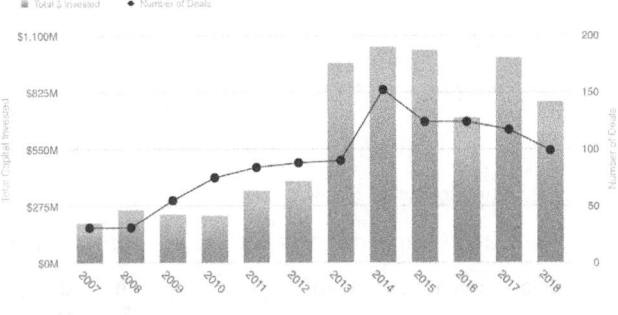

Reported Venture Capital Deal & Dollar Volume For Utah-Based Startups, By Year, Through 2018

Based on angel and seed-stage, early-stage, and late-stage venture capital deals. Excludes private equity. Data is subject to reporting delays, especially for early and seed-stage deals in recent quarters. Data is current through May 13, 2019.

crunchbase news

Wondering what caused this rapid increase in new business in Utah, I stumbled across an article by Savannah Dowling who provided a thoughtful analysis of the situation, arguing that "there are a lot of aspects of Utah that are attractive for entrepreneurs, and the VCs that fund them. Much like in Colorado, operational costs are not as high in Utah, which is an attractive feature for companies and investors. There's also a sense of work-life balance, which many say has led to lower employee attrition rates compared to Silicon Valley companies. Finally, the founders and VCs we spoke to all pointed to one aspect of Utah that is driving entrepreneurship beyond capital, costs, and balance: community. The founders that have paved the way for venture investment in the state are heavily invested in the success of the Utah tech ecosystem as a whole. This supportive culture runs counter to what some consider to be a much more cut-throat culture in the Bay Area. This further solidifies for many budding entrepreneurs in Utah that they don't have to leave to be successful. In fact, it may be better for them to stay."[90]

8,750 MORE MILES WEST

Hugh Mason is an innovator, mentor, entrepreneur, and more. After working as a television producer for BBC, he founded an investment firm and then a production company. He later became an adjunct professor at the prestigious National University of Singapore and brought the concept of start-up acceleration to South- East Asia.

In 2009 he met Wong Meng Weng and took a look at the entrepreneurial ecosystem in Singapore. There was a lot of intellectual capital and financial capital but what was missing was the social capital. Hard to remember now, but back then there was almost no start-up ecosystem in Singapore.

The duo soon realized that in order to help build a community they needed a way for people to connect and learn from each other. So with younger partners, they set up a co-working space called Hackerspace that became incredibly

---

90 Dowling, Savannah. "Utah's Tech Legacy Is Bringing Exits, Funding, And Startups". *Crunchbase News*, May 23, 2019. https://news.crunchbase.com/news/utahs-tech-legacy-is-bringing-exits-funding-and-startups/.

successful. "There was so much energy in the space that we sometimes had to kick people out at 2 a.m." Hugh shares.

In 2010, he helped run some of the first "Start-up Weekends" in the Philippines, Indonesia, and India. Most of them maxed out their capacity of the space. There was a clear need and desire for entrepreneurial know-how, investment and mentoring.

Inspired by demand across the region, the two co-founded JFDI.Asia, the first start-up accelerator in South-East Asia. Initially, it was industry agnostic and had one goal: to get people from idea to investment in one hundred days. This specific goal grew directly out of the needs of the startup companies they had met, at that time in the region. As we have seen so far in this chapter, one should not assume that a developing ecosystem will respond well to approaches that work in those that are more developed. One should look under the surface of what works elsewhere, understand the goal that solution is achieving and then figure out what will achieve the same result in a new context.

At JFDI, the initial idea of building community was never lost. On a weekly basis they organized an open house where anyone interested in innovation and entrepreneurship could come, hang out, and chat. "We did that every single week for five years with over 10,000 people attending in total. In addition to many business partnerships, at least two marriages and four children are direct results of this!" says Hugh.

Entrepreneurship will always be difficult, but it doesn't have to be lonely.

For JFDI's community, social capital is about creating trust, giving before expecting to receive, and respecting local culture. Together, the community learns when it shares stories, says Hugh: "We make sense of a complex reality when we tell stories about the part we can see. Incubators and accelerators have to help founders tell their story and they help the community to see a bigger picture too."

Similarly, Matt Hartman from Betaworks, shares that they "try to foster the ability to communicate to each other and empower people to do so. This increases both the involvement and the well-being of each of the participants."

Constantly we see the human aspect playing an incredible role in the formation of entrepreneurial communities and thus driving economic growth to those areas. The supportive culture, willingness to help and introduce people in the network, openness towards diverse founders, ability to tell one's story, and a determination to build successful companies brings people together to create meaningful change. This metric is hard to quantify, but it nonetheless proves that the Human Approach described in this book works and is increasing in popularity and awareness across the U.S. and the world.

In the following chapters we will explore specific applications of those core tenants in the context of various entrepreneurial support units and how they succeed, or sometimes fail, at building and growing entrepreneurial communities.

KEY TAKEAWAYS:

- People are at the center of entrepreneurial communities, not their businesses.

- Enabling connections between founders and increasing the level of accessibility to entrepreneurial data will naturally lead to stronger communities.

- Areas with intellectual and financial capital are most likely to develop entrepreneurial ecosystems.

- Small and medium sized cities have the potential of becoming the next start-up hubs as the culture of large entrepreneurial clusters strays away from the human values.

CHAPTER 10

CO-WORKING SPACES

—

"You shouldn't focus on why you can't do something, which is what most people do. You should focus on why perhaps you can, and be one of the exceptions."

- STEVE CASE

"Design can be art. Design can be simple. That's why it's so complicated."

–PAUL RAND

"I would rather own little and see the world than own the world and see little of it."

– ALEXANDER SATTLER

We are in the midst of a workplace revolution. For the first time in history, more than half of the world is living in cities — seeking community, purpose, and the opportunity to be a part of something greater than themselves. According to recent estimates by the United Nations, by 2050 over two-thirds of the global population will be based in urban areas.[91] How to navigate the future of work in those mega-cities and pave our way towards a new economy are some of the most important challenges of our time.

Since the first co-working space appeared in 2005, more than 22,000 have opened around the world.[92] With the new millennium came a realization that perhaps nobody needs to be in the office at all. The rise of coffee shops and wireless technology empowered employees to leave their cubicles in the pursuit of a better space to work.

More and more companies are joining the move towards flexible shared office spaces, from solo founders to large enterprises coming to share the same work spaces. Julian Clayton, global head of program management at WeWork, said that "Every enterprise wants to be a start-up and every start-up

91 68% of the world population projected to live in urban areas by 2050. United Nations Department of Economic and Social Affairs. Url: https://www.un.org/development/desa/en/news/population/2018-revision-of-world-urbanization-prospects.html.

92 Number of coworking spaces worldwide from 2005 to 2020. *Statista*. Url: https://www.statista.com/statistics/554273/number-of-coworking-spaces-worldwide/.

wants to be an enterprise. This is why both comfortably find a spot in a co-working space."

On one hand, large companies who lost the small and scrappy mindset want to be in the innovative and vibrant community, while on the other hand, start-ups are looking for the legitimacy and status that a co-working space provides. Those units give their younger members a sense of professionalism and credibility that traditional remote working does not.

So what's all the fuss about?

AROUND THE WORLD

I had the chance to visit co-working spaces on three continents and meet with their community managers in an attempt to understand the shift that is happening in the way people work.

What I noticed over and over again were clean and beautifully designed spaces with lots of natural light, comfortable couches, tall tables, plants, phone booths, coffee machines, coffee, coffee, and more coffee — you start realizing what truly fuels the world's economy. Working there, people of all kinds are armed with a laptop and, you probably guessed, a mug of coffee. No cubicles, almost no private offices, and no cluttered desks with files and paperwork.

I have asked myself if the co-working space is the profession-alization of the coffee shop or the liberalization of the office. I have yet to find an answer.

While in New York City on an industry trip, I had the chance to visit New Lab, an 84,000 square foot facility in the Brooklyn Navy Yard which dates back to 1902 and served as the primary machine shop for every major ship launched during the first and second World Wars. Black steel beams, tall plants, even taller ceilings, and colorful couches is my summary of what felt like the most bad-ass place to work from, home to some of the most radical start-ups in Brooklyn, from Launcher, a metal 3D-printed rocket engines manufacturer, to Farmshelf, an indoor farm designer and producer.

While attending the United Nations USLS in Bangkok, Thailand, I took the opportunity to tour several co-working spaces in the area. At The Hive, I grabbed a coffee and chatted with their community lead, Jeri Littlefair. She shared with me that "It is a perfect deal for the digital nomads. People come here from all over East Asia. Most of our members travel between our locations." The Hive boasts locations in Hong Kong, Singapore, Thailand, Vietnam, Taiwan, and Japan which is pretty impressive. Joining their network is like having an office virtually everywhere in East Asia. The same story applies to co-working networks in all parts of the world.

So is that it? What else brings people to co-working spaces?

The answer is both people and space.

Both are equally correct and could easily steer the conversation towards the "chicken and the egg" dilemma. To save space and time, I'm going to start with the space — pun intended.

SPACE DESIGN

The furniture, office layout, and natural light are just some of the design elements that can help or hinder staff happiness and productivity.

Results from a study conducted by office design company K2 Space suggest that employees consider having access to natural light and a variety of workspace options as absolutely essential in the modern office.[93] These findings support a past report by Human Spaces which found that natural light (42%) and quiet work spaces (22%) were the desired elements in any office.[94]

93 Meeting Expectations – What Employees Really Expect From Their Workplace. *K2 Space.* Url: https://k2space.co.uk/knowledge/meeting-expectations/.
94 Biophilic Design in the Workplace. *Human Spaces.* Url: http://www.usailighting.com/stuff/contentmgr/files/1/c3f5c565a2f50b-69c44dd5d3a12c6fe9/misc/biophilicdesign_humanspaces.pdf.

In the report, the *'biophilia hypothesis'*[95] is mentioned. This study suggests that there is an instinctive bond between human beings and other living systems.[96] In other words, it suggests an inborn affinity — call it love if you want — between humans and the natural world. Therefore, biophilic design is a response to this human need and works to re-establish contact with nature in the unnatural environment.

Contact with nature and design elements which mimic natural materials have been shown to positively impact health, job performance, and concentration while also reducing anxiety and stress. In turn, there are proven links between work environments exhibiting biophilic design and lower staff turnover and absence rates.

Julian Clayton shared that when designing a space, a lot of things are taken into consideration — from ratios of desks, to people working, to the size of the couches, and other specific metrics. At WeWork, every building is a little bit different as it embodies geographically relevant elements. There are some similarities too. One example is that the hallways are purposefully more narrow to make people bump into each other and start conversations. They call those "accidental

95 Wilson, Edward. *Biophilia: The Human Bond With Other Species.* Harvard University Press, 1984.

96 Campbell, Lindsay and Anne Wiesen. *"Restorative Commons: Creating Health And Well-being Through Urban Landscapes".* Gen. Tech. Rep. NRS-P-39 U.S. Department of Agriculture, (2011): 278.

collisions." While visiting their headquarters in New York City, I noticed the tactic in relation to their stairs: narrow while they changed levels and wider as they reached a level — there was even a couch and a coffee table at every level.

An interesting thing to notice is that when standing or sitting at a bar, people tend to congregate around the corners which makes sense because it is easier to look at each other. Julian shared that designers take this into consideration when designing bars and build them with more corners to get people interacting easily.

Doug Chambers, global head of client solutions at WeWork, shared how they use various space types such as meet & greet, work, play, among others, to deliver complex work environments. "It's not just about the physical space, but also about the way we activate it," he says. This is why most if not all co-working spaces have community managers who are working around the clock to make sure people have what they need, curate events, and encourage connections among members.

Overall, it is a combination of designing and running the space. All the clever tricks used in designing work spaces are used primarily to encourage communication among employees in order to drive innovation. It's the duality between the space and its members that one should focus their attention on if they want to understand how to build successful start-up support units.

THE WEWORK EFFECT

What started in February 2010 as a single co-working space in the New York City neighborhood of Soho has grown into a global movement. WeWork reached London in October 2014, and the one hundredth location opened in November 2016 in Berlin, Germany. Nowadays it opens between twenty and forty new locations every month, and as of September 2018 became Manhattan's biggest holder of real estate.[97]

Why has it become so popular?

There are many benefits to joining such units. According to their 2019 Global Impact Report, WeWork members not only save money on office expenses but their companies grow and thrive, with 54% of members crediting WeWork with accelerating their company's growth.[98]

---

97 Morris, Keiko and Eliot Brown. "WeWork Surpasses JPMorgan as Biggest Occupier of Manhattan Office Space". *Wall Street Journal*, Sep. 18, 2018. https://www.wsj.com/articles/wework-surpasses-jp-morgan-as-biggest-occupier-of-manhattan-office-space-1537268401.

98 2019 Global Impact Report. *WeWork*. Url: https://www.wework.com/newsroom/posts/2019-global-impact-report.

Furthermore, member firms attract up to ten times more applications for an open job position.[99] The office is so much more vibrant that people want to work for those companies. Leslie Kurkijian Crowe, chief people officer at TripActions, shares how "WeWork has enabled us to hire great talent that we otherwise wouldn't have been able to. Instead of being siloed in our Palo Alto headquarters, we now recruit the very best talent in cities all over the globe."[100] Their firm operates in five WeWork locations across the U.S., U.K., and the Netherlands.

Nathan Kigenyi, founder and creative director of Capture Create Media anda member of a WeWork in Washington, D.C. says, "Our studio is strategically positioned, giving us the opportunity to showcase our work in real time. This advantage allowed us to grow our business by 75 percent in the first year."[101]

Rachel Wilson, founder of the L.A. based marketing firm Lady Rebranded, says that "50 percent of my clients come from WeWork, or secondary and tertiary relationships that began at WeWork."[102] Furthermore, co-working spaces help new businesses such as Rachel's make a positive impression

---

99 Ibid.
100 Ibid.
101 Ibid.
102 Ibid.

on potential clientele by offering amenities way past what those start-ups could afford on their own.

In major U.S. cities, one in eight first-time entrepreneurs are building their businesses in WeWork, 83% of them being in high-growth sectors such as technology, creative and professional services, and advanced manufacturing.[103]

In a *Harvard Business Review* article, researchers from the University of Michigan share that workers benefit from co-working spaces more than traditional offices. "They experience greater levels of flexibility and thriving (defined as vitality and learning at work), a greater ability to network, as well as a stronger sense of community."[104]

Contrary to what could be believed, their findings indicate that the WeWork brand identity doesn't dilute the identity of the organizations housed in their space. Rather "people experience positive outcomes when their work environment aligns with their company's brand messaging and values."

Arun Sundararajan, a professor at New York University's Stern School of Business and the author of *The Sharing*

---

103 Ibid.
104 Bacevice, Peter, Gretchen Spreitzer, Hilary Hendricks and Daniel Davis. "How Coworking Spaces Affect Employees' Professional Identities". *Harvard Business Review*, Apr. 17, 2019. https://hbr.org/2019/04/how-coworking-spaces-affect-employees-professional-identities.

Economy shares that "WeWork has created the physical-world equivalent of a digital platform, creating value by imprinting design onto physical space, which leads to network effects at both the individual and institutional levels. Its global constellation of companies and entrepreneurs allow members to tap into and realize value from these economic spillovers, within their local communities and across cities."

The impact is not confined to the co-working space but rather spreads to the surrounding community. Rahm Emanuel, former mayor of Chicago, shares how "In Chicago, start-ups, small businesses, and entrepreneurs can access a strong support network and connect with an established business community across every sector of our well-diversified economy. WeWork has been an important partner in helping Chicago accelerate economic growth, create jobs for residents, and turn innovative ideas into successful companies."

* * *

And now, what for a long time seemed to be only reserved for the start-up world, suddenly became available for the large enterprises too.

According to the same Global Impact Report, over one-third of the "Global Fortune 500" are WeWork members, having joined in search of global scale and flexibility, access to talent, and community with 49% of enterprise WeWork members saying that WeWork has helped them enter new markets.

Enterprises can now get custom made floors, or sometimes whole buildings, through WeWork's extension called Powered by We. Their winning strategy is so good that other companies want to be in spaces designed by them. WeWork now runs an entire building for IBM in New York, the Airbnb's office in Berlin, and Amazon's office in Boston. Microsoft, Salesforce, UBS, and even the U.S. Air Force also have teams that call WeWork home.

Julian Clayton shared that when designing a space, the first thing they ask about is the vertical or verticals the company will operate in. Since everyone has their own needs, they take the role of a consultant in this space. Bringing data from possibly the largest, most varied, and most precise data set of employee behavior in a space, they are able to help other enterprises reach the same standard of office space as their start-up competitors. It is worth noting that the enterprise arm was almost nonexistent a couple years ago and now it's a big part of WeWork's business and revenue.

The WeWork effect is not only the special sauce of its creator anymore, but rather a world-wide phenomenon characterized by a focus on the design of the physical space in which people work and the community that forms around it. It's beautifully designed, modern, collaborative, fresh, and vibrant.

IT'S HUMAN

Over and over again we see incredible results as companies migrate towards share office spaces and intermingle in a creative and dynamic community. The twenty-first century, in the midst of the digital revolution, is offering the opportunity to reconnect with our human analog self and interact with others the old way: in real face-to face-conversation. "It's all about community. Co-working spaces provide you with the ability to be around like minded people" shares Doug. After all, WeWork's success, as well as other units', are built around the concept of community.

Tim Brown in his book *Change by Design* brings us to the reality: "To be creative, a place does not have to be crazy, kooky, and located in northern California. What is a prerequisite is an environment — social but also spatial — in which people know they can experiment, take risks, and explore the full range of their faculties. The physical and psychological spaces of an organization work in tandem to define the effectiveness of the people within it."[105]

---

105 Brown, Tim. *Change by Design: How Design Thinking Transforms Organizations and Inspires Innovation*. HarperBusiness, 2009.

KEY TAKEAWAYS:

- Co-working spaces have made an incredible impact in the twenty-first century because of their timing with a massive change in the workplace culture.

- Spaces play an important role in how companies operate and much thought has to be put into designing work environments that align with the firm's culture.

- The goal of an office should be to make people more collaborative and more productive, thus increasing the chances of breakthrough innovation.

CHAPTER 11

INCUBATORS & ACCELERATORS

———

"Diligence is the mother of good luck."

- BENJAMIN FRANKLIN

"The value of an idea lies in the using of it."

- THOMAS EDISON

"The best way to do something 'lean' is to gather a tight group of people, give them very little money, and very little time."

- BOB KLEIN

"I wish I could say that Paul, Robert, Trevor, and I knew this would be one of the big ones when we interviewed Drew and Arash on April 21, 2007. They were the first interview of the day, at 8:30am. Though it was a long time ago, I remember we all agreed that they seemed good, and it was an easy decision to fund them. Trevor had already looked at the software and was impressed by it. When Drew applied to YC, he applied as a single founder. After we invited him to interviews, Paul sent him an email suggesting he'd be better off with a co-founder. By interviews, a few weeks later, he'd found Arash. That worked out well. Drew and Arash spent the summer of 2007 writing code. In those days there were a lot of file storage and syncing services, but none of them worked very well. The Dropbox founders were determined from the very beginning to win by making a product that was better than anything else. Little did I know back then what a momentous check this one would be: that 11 years later, Dropbox would be the first Y-Combinator company to go public," shares Jessica Livingston, co-founder of Y-Combinator, in an article on the accelerator's blog.[106]

When reading Jessica's recount of the very beginning of Dropbox, it is hard not to wonder what the famous four saw in Drew and Arash that led them to support a seemingly

---

106 Livingston, Jessica. "Congrats Dropbox!". *Y Combinator Blog*, Mar. 23, 2018. https://blog.ycombinator.com/congratsdropbox/.

boring idea of storing and synchronizing files online. It seems that they didn't buy into the idea of a specific software product, but rather invested in a talented duo who would masterfully execute any idea.

Jess Williamson talks about how after her experience with the Techstars accelerator she will never underestimate anyone she meets. "As an investor you are constantly making decisions on who is worthy of your capital and who is not but that is always a subjective and imperfect process, no matter how much we try to justify it with metrics. So many more founders I would want to have selected and couldn't."

It is important to recognize that there are so many people who will get a "no" but are still amazing entrepreneurs. The selection process itself is flawed because it is human. In recent years, on the investor side of accelerators we see a larger focus on the pair of co-founders than on the idea itself. This is one of the effects of what I described as the Human Approach. Though this is not necessarily a bad thing, it is a reality people need to be aware of in order to properly understand the way entrepreneurial support programs operate.

* * *

For clarification purposes, let's define what we are talking about. Ryan Kushner does an amazing job at introducing the two concepts we will be tackling in this chapter:

- "An accelerator is a program that accepts companies (or ideas or people) in batches – usually called classes or cohorts. It traditionally culminates in a demo day where companies pitch themselves to potential customers, partners, investors, and employees. There is generally a cash-for-equity swap, but not all the time. The training is intensive, and the program invests a lot of time in the companies. Because of this companies tend to be later stage."[107]

- "An incubator is generally for companies at an earlier stage, and it accepts them in a continuous flow, space/capacity allowing. Incubators act a lot like co-working spaces by charging for desk space (and not doing equity deals), but they are more invested in their companies' success. They offer things like skills training, connections to mentors and investors, and an aligned community."[108]

107 Kushner, Ryan. *Accelerate This!: A Super Not Boring Guide To Startup Accelerators And Clean Energy Entrepreneurship*. CreateSpace Independent Publishing Platform, 2018.
108 Ibid.

New York University economist and researcher Ian Hathaway shares in a *Harvard Business Review* article that "the confusion is real, including within the start-up sector itself. In fact, of the nearly 700 U.S.-based organizations that were identified as an 'accelerator' or 'accelerator/incubator' or similar — either through self-identification or through leading investor databases — I could confirm these four criteria in fewer than one-third of them. In other words, two of every three 'accelerators' are not in fact accelerators, based on this criterion."[109]

The naming may be, to some extent, irrelevant as we discuss the large variety that exists among those support units.

SO WHY JOIN INCUBATORS AND ACCELERATORS?

Mike Wright and Israel Drori mentioned in their latest research book *Accelerators* that "Young or new ventures increasingly choose to join business assistance programs as entrepreneurs are facing high levels of ambiguity during their search for solutions to problems that are still imperfectly defined." [110]Overall, founders affiliate with such programs because they need more support than they could get in a

109 Hathaway, Ian. "What Startup Accelerators Really Do". *Harvard Business Review*, Mar. 01, 2016. https://hbr.org/2016/03/what-startup-accelerators-really-do.

110 Wright, Mike and Israel Dori. *Accelerators: Successful Venture Creation and Growth*. Edward Elgar Pub, 2018.

co-working space for a longer period of time than they could get in a bootcamp program.

There are many advantages to joining such units. Apart from the standard resources such as office space and administrative services, programs across the world offer a variety of specialized resources too. Most of them are dependent on the skills of the unit managers and employees while some depend on the quality of the network built.

One of the critical reasons founders join such programs is the specialized knowledge of experts in their industry. This is one of the reasons more and more programs decide to focus on specific business areas in which to amass great expertise. A 2016 report by Gust showed that "The global acceleration landscape is increasingly moving towards verticalization, with 57.5% of accelerators running programs focused on a particular industry or sector niche. This trend is likely to continue as regional start-up ecosystems continue to mature. This is a very positive development because verticalized accelerators generally bring more value to start-ups through more qualified acceleration teams, larger pools of quality mentors within the industry, and close corporate ties to related markets."[111]

---

111 Global Accelerator Report 2016. *Gust*. Url: http://gust.com/accelerator_reports/2016/global/.

* * *

At HAX, the world's largest hardware accelerator, head of design Noel Joyce shares that they "deliver a huge amount of expert industrial design and engineering help." With over 50,000 square feet in Shenzhen, China, and a lot of people on staff to help founders execute on their ideas, they spend a lot of time on problem solving and iterative design. It seems that there are no technical questions that cannot be answered.

"By being based in Shenzhen we can operate at an incredible speed. We can take the elevator or cross the street and have 20 variants of the same component an hour later," says Noel. This became HAX's key differentiator and you can see the incredible difference between the first day and three months after a founder joins the program. The human-centered design, precision, and attention to details impresses the investors and produces great returns, as we have seen in Chapter 8 with the food start-up Nomiku.

In a conversation with Cyril Ebersweiler, founder and managing director of HAX, he argues that his program is not quite an accelerator, rather it is more committed and involved: "We accelerate products. There is no demo day. You stay until you ship the product." When asked then what would be the difference between HAX and start-up studio he laughs, "Well, it depends. At the end of the day we are essentially a co-founder. We are with them in the very first months of the start-up — all of us. Everybody is a fucking co-founder a this point, we are all on board."

The HAX experience is the way it is because of people like Cyril and Noel putting their heart and soul into the success of their companies. Noel shares that "There is this feeling that each project is our own. We have skin in the game and that makes us go the extra mile for our founders." It appears to be the human involvement that characterizes the success of all those resources — it enhances all the other support offered.

One of the questions you might have is: are accelerators actually having an impact on the growth of those companies?

Data suggest that they do, and the trend holds true for other entrepreneurial support programs as well. According to a recent study by PitchBook, more than one-third of start-ups who ended up raising a series A have graduated from an accelerator.[112] The graph below, put together by Ryan Kushner, shows the staggering difference an entrepreneurial support unit makes in the evolution of a start-up.[113]

---

112 Tom, Mikey. "One-third of U.S. startups that raised a Series A in 2015 went through an accelerator". *PitchBook*, Feb. 5, 2016. https://pitchbook.com/news/articles/one-third-of-us-startups-that-raised-a-series-a-in-2015-went-through-an-accelerator.

113 Kushner, Ryan. *Accelerate This!: A Super Not Boring Guide To Startup Accelerators And Clean Energy Entrepreneurship*. CreateSpace Independent Publishing Platform, 2018.

Are Accelerated Ventures More Likely To Grow?

Difference in Percentage of Participated and Rejected
With Positive One-Year Changes

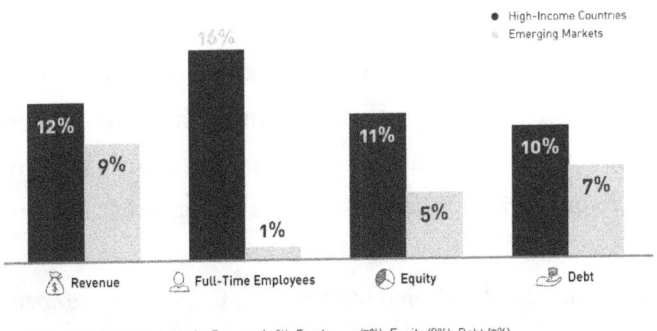

- ● High-Income Countries
- ○ Emerging Markets

12%	16%	11%	10%
9%	1%	5%	7%

Revenue   Full-Time Employees   Equity   Debt

Percentages for the full sample: Revenue (10%); Employees (7%); Equity (8%); Debt (9%)

Source: GALI (2017). Accelerating Startups in Emerging Markets: Insights from 43 Programs.
Note: Data based on study of 43 programs.

* * *

One could ask how are those units able to drive so much value in such a limited time?

Susan Cohen challenges viewing that as a problem and writes in her research that "Paradoxically, the limited duration of accelerator programs increases the influence the programs have on portfolio ventures. An accelerator director who had been making angel investments before he started his accelerator explained that, as an angel, he was frustrated by the limited contact and influence he had with ventures, often seeing founders only at quarterly board meetings."[114] The

114 Cohen, Susan. *"What Do Accelerators Do? Insights from Incubators and Angels"*. Innovations: Technology, Governance, Globalization

limited duration of the accelerator artificially forces intensity and urgency in delivering all resources available.

Repeatedly, we see support units as a way of bringing people together, much more than the sum of their non-human resources. The programs bound to win are the ones who are able to put their founders first and help them win.

Things such as educational resources for founders, time spent discussing and debating the entrepreneurial journey, and the mindset of the entrepreneur will aid in the development of the founder as a person and hence their business too.

Juanita Gonzalez-Uribe, assistant professor at the London School of Economics, along with Michael Leatherbee, assistant professor at Pontificia Universidad Católica de Chile, write in their paper that "Regarding the policy design of ecosystem accelerator programs, if the objective is to accelerate start-ups, our results suggest that more resources should be allocated toward combining basic services with entrepreneurship schooling, rather than providing basic services on their own. This conclusion is particularly valid for programs that focus on young founders and early-stage start-ups."[115]

8, no. 3 (2013): 19-25.

115 Gonzalez-Uribe, Juanita and Michael Leatherbee. *"The Effects of Business Accelerators on Venture Performance: Evidence from Start-Up Chile"*. The Review of Financial Studies 31, no. 4 (2018): 1566–1603.

When looking at flourishing programs, the success rate of educational resources confirms every time. Kat Manalac, one of the partners of the famous Y-Combinator, shared in an interview with Ryan Kushner that "The main thing we focus on is founders, because we understand that ideas change. We can't marry the idea, so we really focus on whether founders can execute. We think, 'Does this company have the potential to become a billion-dollar company?' Or, if it's a nonprofit, 'Can it impact millions of people, and how we can help them do that?'."[116]

In the words of Hugh Mason, co-founder and CEO of JFDI. Asia, "Accelerators are more like Greek Theaters, it's a community activity." Bringing people together and making them realize what they can do together should be a principal focus. We need to move away from what he calls the "car wash perspective": you get dirty entrepreneurs, you add shampoo, and you take them out investor ready — similar to the perspective some have about universities, where we insert children and get back educated adults.

These are just some of the hundreds of examples available of how entrepreneurial support units are adopting a more human approach to entrepreneurship, increasingly focusing

---

116 Kushner, Ryan. *Accelerate This!: A Super Not Boring Guide To Startup Accelerators And Clean Energy Entrepreneurship.* CreateSpace Independent Publishing Platform, 2018.

on the development of the founder in the context of a broader community. In the end, start-ups are just a collection of humans working together towards a common goal.

The rewards of such a change in perspective goes beyond the founders to the supporters too. Jess Williamson shares that start-up incubation and acceleration is a rewarding business not just financially. During her first demo day at Springboard, the predecessor of Techstars, all founders were able to get on stage and gracefully present the progress that they had made and articulate their company's value in the market. "When running an accelerator, you'll get feedback from all mentors and people love to be critical and skeptical. When you can overcome all the skepticism and be proud of all your companies, you will truly enjoy the process," she shares. The story repeated every year — "I was excited every single time." When they had their demo day for Techstars in Adelaide, Australia and Cape Town, South Africa, everyone was warning against establishing those programs in those locations and claiming that no innovation was going to spring. "We proved them wrong. We had entrepreneurs with amazing products and services. The excitement never wore off."

CORPORATE PARTNERSHIPS

Keith Berry has always worked in finance. During his executive MBA at Wharton, he became very interested in entrepreneurship classes. With an established family, small children, mortgage, and all of his other responsibilities, he didn't seem to be in a good position to go and do a start-up . But life is interesting and offers you opportunities when you least expect it. I got a chance to meet him at a conference when he shared the following story:

> "One day, the president of Moody's Analytics, the company he worked for, called him in his office. "Listen Keith, we're worried about the disruption coming from fintech start-ups so we need a way to innovate faster and intentional" he said. Keith was about to reply when his boss continued, "We have decided to establish a start-up unit, an internal accelerator, and we want you to lead it." At first, Keith did not enjoy the idea. Why give up running a 100 million business with a team of over 300 people and join a brand new project? "Look, just give us more money and relief on the margins required and we will innovate internally" he replied to his boss, but the decision was made and an offer was on the table. Keith was persuaded that he should try this and took the lead on what is now known as the Moody's Analytics Accelerator."

In such a unit, acceleration is done more purposefully than in a normal accelerator. Similarly, you have a group of product people, business and engineers, and employ a lean start-up approach, but the partnerships with start-ups have to lead to different opportunities for win-win situations. The host company is usually a client of the start-ups it is accelerating. The rest of the time, it'll be their owner.

Bottom line, both parties do well. Start-ups get access to a well known brand, distribution capabilities, sales, and marketing forces, but most importantly they get access to customers. In the case of Moody's Analytics, we are talking about financial institutions, such as big banks, that are known to be very conservative about vendors. This is a huge advantage for a start-up who would never pass the due diligence imposed by the large corporations to mitigate vendor risk.

The result of the partnership is and should be a new product, even though normally the start-up already has a product when joining the accelerator. Corporate programs like Moody's focus on early and mid-stage ventures as it is harder to work with mature start-ups — they are becoming a big company themselves and thus leave less opportunities for a win-win situation. On the other end, it would be hard to work with a very small start-up since there is not enough material to work with. "We don't want to turn a start-up into our outsourced technology development unit. Can we bring data analytics and distribution channels to jointly develop a product? If not, it's a no go," shares Keith.

Research seems to agree. The 2016 report issued by Gust identified an increased collaboration between accelerators and corporations. "On the one hand, this is because corporations are discovering that accelerators are an efficient and effective way to engage with start-ups. On the other hand, accelerators understand that corporations can help them fund operations in the short-to-medium term (exits are often far out). They improve the prospects of their portfolio companies that can potentially sell to, raise funds from, or be acquired by these corporations," said Miklos Grof, co-author of this report.[117]

* * *

At Techstars, Jess Williamson revealed that they initially didn't have any corporate partners but rather accelerators that were run by Techstars employees. The model soon evolved to recognize that there was a need for corporate start-up partnerships. "Anything from distribution channels, partnership opportunities, investments and industry insights are attractive sells for emerging start-ups," says Jess. On the corporate side, the resistance to change is mediated through such units and the company can more quickly get a grasp of new technologies and other innovations.

---

117 Global Accelerator Report 2016. *Gust.* Url: http://gust.com/accelerator_reports/2016/global/.

One of the bigger issues comes in the post-program implementation of the start-up driven products due to stiffness in management and the aforementioned resistance to change. "This problem varies a lot based on the leadership of the corporate and how much are they able to recognize this issue," she shares. Some companies are better than others at doing so. She continues to share that "We had a great experience with Barclay's. They were very good at recognizing what the challenges were and changing internally to fast track deals with start-ups through the accelerator."

ONLINE V.S. OFFLINE

After doing research on what support systems drive the development of innovation districts, Rachel Jaffe was asked by her mentors why she doesn't go ahead and try to build something herself to help other entrepreneurs get support. "So, um, after a lot of talking, I decided to enter into a pitch competition in Austin at SXSW and I actually won third place just with drawings on a piece of paper," she recalls.

Upon her return, she got back in contact with her friend Sal from undergrad and together they decided to spend the next two years learning how to code. At first, all they knew was how to do basic websites, but Rachel really wanted to build a mobile app. She recalls thinking, "Let's at least try to build something," and in about three weeks they built a template based on Tinder where pretty much the only thing one could do was see one or two sentences about an idea and either swipe right or swipe left.

They passed it around to a lot of people and most of them loved it. They spent an entire year building the first version of Adjacent with the goal that people can go anywhere and find a co-founder for their idea. "At the time we released it, it was so buggy and it was so broken that no one can use it. We got terrible reviews on it but we also got a lot of people saying this is still really, really awesome," she recalls.

A year later Adjacent, a virtual incubator, was released to the public. Now it allows anyone with an idea to put it up on the app along with other things that they need to make their idea become a reality. The app then connects them with other people who can help. One can also search through different ideas in the app and give feedback and in turn get crowd-sourced feedback on their ideas too.

Whether calling Adjacent a Facebook for entrepreneurs or a Tinder for entrepreneurs, one thing is for sure: it electronically brings people together to work on ideas. Does that make it worthy of the "incubator" title? That is debatable. As we have seen in this chapter, more resources are needed in order to be able to drive meaningful support to entrepreneurs. Adjacent and similar programs cover the first stage of the start-up building process but cannot offer a whole incubator solution because they are missing the human aspect to it.

With more and more programs offering online components or being completely internet-based, the question now stands as to which of the options makes more sense in today's business environment. Could online incubators and accelerators be the future of the industry? Can we trade depth for convenience?

I asked start-up accelerator expert Ryan Kushner to provide his perspective on this matter and he brought up the issue of trust. "With funding being an integral part of the process we need to ask ourselves whether people will be willing to invest without meeting the founder in person? You will always need an analog component to the digital program," he shares. After all, working in-person is more time efficient: it builds trust and communities faster.

WHERE DOES ONE START TO BUILD A GREAT ACCELERATOR OR INCUBATOR?

When asked this question, Cyril Ebersweiler cynically suggests, "I would tell people to not build accelerators in the first place. The world needs more genuine support for entities that are truly wanting to move 100% of their companies to market." The reality is that entrepreneurship is not about gambling to sell a company for a billion dollars, but about driving sustainable value to customers and making a profit along the way. The entrepreneurs are the customers of those programs. An accelerator or incubator manager should understand that before starting. They need to figure out how to make money as a start-up unit too. The business model is critical and sometimes overlooked.

Jess Williamson suggests starting with the question of "Why do you want to start an accelerator program?" People think that there is a magic formula: ten start-ups for three months + co-working space + funding + partners + mentors + workshops + demo day = accelerator. This is undermining the whole human aspect of the program. "Accelerators are creating a strong sense of community where individuals are going to trust, help and respect each other," she says.

One should ask themselves if they are bringing the right kind of mentors who will be willing to provide valuable help. Great accelerators and incubators are designed with alignment between stakeholders. They find people with a good understanding of the industry and provide a framework for them to create amazing inventions. They are geographically relevant and are able to support start-ups all through product and service delivery. Most importantly, they bring people together and encourage them to meaningfully exchange ideas, build trust and collaborate.

KEY TAKEAWAYS:

- The process of entrepreneurial support is naturally sub-jective and biased. This could be viewed as a problem, but it also creates the opportunity for genuine human interaction to occur.

- The expertise of incubators' and accelerators' employees is one of the biggest aspects that draws entrepreneurs towards a specific program.

- Most incubators and accelerators offer similar resources. The defining factor will be the involvement of the unit in the development of the founders as people, and thus the development of their products, services, and businesses.

- Corporate partnerships work because they create win-win situations. One side breaks the internal innovation barrier while the other finds paths of acceleration.

- The very act of helping founders reach their potential is highly rewarding for the mentors involved in the process.

CHAPTER 12

START-UP STUDIOS

———

"It is always the practice of wise people to reserve something for tomorrow, and not venture all their eggs in one basket."

- SANCHO PANZA

"I skate to where the puck is going to be, not where it has been."

- WAYNE GRETZY

"You don't learn to walk by following rules. You learn by doing and falling over."

- RICHARD BRANSON

"It is not the critic who counts: not the man who points out how the strong man stumbles or where the doer of deeds could have done better. The credit belongs to the man who is actually in the arena, whose face is marred by dust and sweat and blood, who strives valiantly, who errs and comes up short again and again, because there is no effort without error or shortcoming, but who knows the great enthusiasms, the great devotions, who spends himself for a worthy cause; who, at the best, knows, in the end, the triumph of high achievement, and who, at the worst, if he fails, at least he fails while daring greatly, so that his place shall never be with those cold and timid souls who knew neither victory nor defeat." You may or may not recognize this from the famous speech given by former president Theodore Roosevelt on April 23rd, 1910 in Paris -- "Citizenship in a Republic."[118]

But what does it have to do with a chapter about start-up studios?

Well, this passage is the philosophy statement of Archimedes Labs, a Palo Alto based start-up studio founded by Keith Teare and Mike Arrington, the famous duo behind Tech-Crunch. You might be wondering right now:

---

118 "The Man in The Arena" at the Theodore Roosevelt Center at Dickinson State University. Url: https://www.theodorerooseveltcenter.org/Learn-About-TR/TR-Encyclopedia/Culture-and-Society/Man-in-the-Arena.aspx#top.

WHAT IS A START-UP STUDIO?

If you are confused, let me assure you that you are not alone. Originally introduced in 1996 by Bill Gross founding Idealab, the concept of a start-up studio didn't really get enough traction until 2008. Prior to 2007, there really wasn't any such thing as a pre-seed investment, and with the rapid evolution of the investment world start-up studios found a niche as a reaction to that VC environment. Subsequent years saw a rapid rise in the number of studios popping out all over the world, from Australia to South Africa and from Europe to the Americas. Money did follow, with over four billion dollars being raised by venture builders since 2010, investments increasing 48% year-over-year.

Start-up studios, also known as venture builders, start-up factories, start-up foundries, or venture production studios, are the new players in the entrepreneurial world and are taking the industry by storm. Operating more or less like a start-up-factory, they are working on multiple different ideas, creating prototypes, testing them, and based on the feedback, either continue with the project or move to another one.

A start-up studio should not be confused with neither accelerators nor incubators, as the main purpose of a studio is to continually create start-ups using a creative and efficient infrastructure. Incubators and accelerators provide support in a later stage of development, while start-up studios are themselves the first stage when there is just a concept or an idea, no team, no CEO, and no business model. Successful examples include Obvious Ventures, who built Medium and Change.org, HVF Labs, who built Affirm, Betaworks, who built Giphy and Bitly, and Science, who built Dollar Shave Club.

Think of them as the entrepreneurial cousin of the Hollywood studio. After all, they are creating a story, leveraging internal writers, directors, production crew, and hiring external actors and other staff as needed. They are responsible for the whole creation process of the movie, developing a marketing strategy, filming, producing, and launching the final product. All of this while having multiple movies in the pipeline at different stages of development.

Jules Ehrhardt, founder of FKTRY and former co-owner of digital product studio utswo, mentions that "the definition does not really matter. It's a vessel for an assembly of smart people, well-versed in making things and starting companies, working out every and any which way they can best apply their energy, experience, network and knowledge."[119]

119 Crook, Jordan. "FKTRY Wants To Be A New Type Of Startup Studio". *Techcrunch*, 2018. https://techcrunch.com/2018/05/17/fctry-wants-to-be-a-new-type-of-startup-studio/.

Start-up studios can now be found all around the world. A team of MBA students led by Professor Eric Koester for Kingmaker Labs at the University of Georgetown found that a majority of the studios are located in the United States and Europe. However, studios are spread throughout the world and continue to rise up in different countries such as South Africa, Russia, China, and others.[120]

SO.. WHO AND HOW?

Ben Elowitz is the managing Director of Madrona Venture Labs (MVL), a Seattle based start-up studio focused on machine learning and artificial intelligence. He recalls his early years as a kid, when the world "entrepreneur" was looked down upon and mostly viewed as an unemployed person. Now a successful entrepreneur, he is rewriting that old definition and joining a group of many who are doing so across the globe.

"We now see entrepreneurs on covers of magazines portrayed as superheroes, people with crazy ideas that ended up working and becoming profitable. We have been witnessing for a whole generation now the legitimization of start-ups and entrepreneurship as a whole," he says.

---

120 Startup Studio 2.0: An Industry Overview And Analysis Of The Next Phase Of Developing Startup Studios. *KML Research*, 2015.

This has become a meaningful and achievable career, with many people around the world viewing it as the height of success. If building businesses became a career, why not become really good at it? In Ben's words, "start-up studios represent the huge professionalization of entrepreneurship."

So how do you become good at building start-ups?

Well, it is worth noting that most start-up studios have been founded by previously successful multi time entrepreneurs who were able to gather a core group of specialists with industry experience to develop a replicable venture creation model. They have an appreciation for the process of creation, rather than just being investor oriented.

Madrona Venture Labs placed a bet on the Seattle talent in order to drive its development. The North West has seen an incredible tech talent boom in the past twenty years, but start-up communities have formed predominantly on the Californian coast. Big companies such as Amazon and Microsoft developed an amazing pool of candidates for entrepreneurial projects, but failed to aid in the development of that ecosystem. MVL's tight partnership with Madrona Venture Group gave the studio much more than just access to a really important network of people; it gave them a fresh set of eyes in the decisional process. This allowed them to basically live in two worlds: one of creative entrepreneurship and one of judgmental venture capital.

It is of the utmost important to make sure you are carefully deciding where to concentrate your efforts. The due diligence process can be applied in the early creation stage of the start-up and thus save the studio countless hours of wasted work and money. Ben mentions that they take this process very seriously at Madrona Venture Labs and will always be searching for market demand, product validation, market size, and customer acquisition cost early in the development pipeline.

* * *

Talking about the usual workflow at MVL, Ben shared that in a regular year they would have played with over one hundred ideas, digging deeper into ten to twenty of them, and spinning out only three. The ideas can come from anywhere, both from exterior individuals and from inside the studio. Once an idea is in, a basic due diligence process begins by taking a look at the total market size and value proposition, with a goal of estimating whether or not there would be enough interest in the idea if it were built. If it passes the first test,a team will be formed around the idea, usually consisting of at least one developer, a product manager, and a market researcher. The validation stage can take anywhere from a couple weeks to several months. At the end of this period, a decision has to be made if the idea has enough market potential that it is worth pursuing as a start-up. If the second test is passed, a full team will be assembled in order to accelerate the growth, develop financial models, and get a full pitch deck ready to look for venture funding.

You may be asking yourself why would a studio needs that external founder to collaborate on some of the projects if they have this whole process in place. One answer is the passion that comes along with a founder. Building a business is a hard job, and many times stressful and unrewarding. During those periods, spirit-heading a team is backed only by strong motivation and desire to succeed.

This is achieved by people who are wired to their ventures, putting all of their energy into them.

The caveat is that those people usually lack all the resources they need to make their dreams a reality, which is where the start-up studio comes in. Jason Ford, partner and Chief Innovation Officer of Saturn V which is a start-up studio in Austin, Texas, shared that he "came to the start-up studio model with the idea of a broken, unfair, and not diverse system in mind, wanting a better solution to this."

Seen as the ultimate co-founder, a studio is able to provide resources and man-hours in order to get those ideas to the market. At the same time, on the studio end we run into a problem of bandwidth. There is no single person who can be an active co-founder for so many start-ups. An organization could theoretically fill this role much easier without spreading the co-founder too thin. VC-backable start-ups require frequent decisions and constant action. This can be achieved only if every project receives the necessary attention.

So how many people are usually part of a start-up studio?

At Betaworks, the number of people depends on how many companies they are building at the time. They do hire constantly as a result of this flexible mindset. In 2012, they brought in eight hackers in residence with the goal of spinning out eight companies. The following year, they didn't start any new projects, but rather worked on building the ones they started the year before. There is no magical formula for how many people should be part of a start-up studio, but one should carefully decide how many projects can they handle and staff those projects accordingly.

Who are the people fit to join start-up studios?

Kevin Leneway, head of engineering at Pioneer Square Labs, shares that they are looking for people who are not just good at writing code or design but who are well-rounded and able to think holistically about the process of building a new product or start-up. "Sometimes developers want to solve problems with what they know best: writing code. But the question is how can we creatively solve the problem, not just by writing software for it?" he says. PSL's twenty-three-person team is a combination of former operators, start-up investors, engineers, designers, and business analysts.

Every start-up idea has such different risks associated with it that without a diverse team and a proper resource play-book to know what you need and when you need it, failure is guaranteed.

In regards to the founders who associate themselves with start-up studios to co-build ventures, the stories vary. Ben Gilbert, co-founder of PSL, shares that they "anticipated when we started that the studio model will be incredibly appealing for people who were inexperienced entrepreneurs. We were surprised by how popular it was with people who were entrepreneurs in the past. They wanted to join a company who was already a little of the ground because that was the stage they enjoyed working on, not the super early idea validation stage."

* * *

An interesting phenomenon that is worth mentioning is the migration of staff from the studio to the newly built company. To some extent, this is already built in the model since a studio will have to hire that person anyway, either for the company or the studio.

MVL sees this as a source of value for the companies they spin out. "When people join start-up studios, they do so because they want the ability to work on multiple things and learn. It follows naturally that they will at some point go full time in a start-up they are creating," Ben Elowitz shared. Some start-ups have a hard time finding talent, so this comes as a blessing for them, receiving some high quality full time employees exactly when needed.

At Betaworks, Matt Hartman, former Director of Seed Investments and now a partner at Betaworks Ventures, has a more resigned perspective: "The migration of talent is neither a blessing not a problem, it is a reality. Someone is going to run that company and we won't just hand it out to someone. We are very transparent when making those transitions showing roughly how the equity going to look like. This is very specific to this model." As we will see later in the chapter in the case of Giphy, as the project started to take off, they were growing so quickly that they had to pull a lot of people into the team and most of them were from inside Betaworks.

An even more surprising example comes from Saturn V where Jason Ford, one of the partners, ended up joining one of the spinout companies. Jason is now the vice president of software engineering at ICON3D, an Austin-based construction technologies company dedicated to revolutionizing home-building and making dignified housing the standard for people throughout the world. Using proprietary 3D printing robotics, software, and advanced materials, ICON is solving a range of problems in the contemporary building industry. Jason's plan is to stay at the firm for three to five years before returning again to the studio. Interestingly enough, the other two partners are also working full time for spin out companies and have made plans of returning in the near future.

Evan Williams shares a similar story. In 2006 after launching Blogger, he co-founded start-up studio Obvious Corp. which later built Twitter. Soon after realizing the potential of that idea, Williams wound down operations at Obvious and joined Twitter full time. After stepping down as CEO of Twitter, Williams relaunched Obvious with Twitter co-founder Biz Stone. Once again, when Williams found his next big idea- the blogging platform Medium- he pulled back from Obvious to focus on Medium full time.

WHY BUILD A START-UP STUDIO?

The concept of a start-up studio brings with it a plethora of benefits. The most obvious one is the increase in speed and the decrease in risk. The ability to rapidly develop and provide prototypes of products while developing multiple start-ups at once is a game changer in the field.

This speed is critical in making sure non-competitive projects are weeded out fast and the right projects get enough attention. This not only reduces the waste of time and talent while bringing high potential ideas to surface, but is doing so reducing the overall risk of the portfolio. The fast validation cycle increases the chances of success of all projects targeted by the studio.

"With each company, you're applying for a seven to ten year journey at the very least," says Max Levchin, who has launched two companies out of HVF, including the fertility app Glow and the financial services start-up, Affirm. "Now, the recent trend is a bunch of people who have had success in the past are asking themselves, 'Why does it have to be one idea per decade?'"

Jason Ford, from Saturn V, shares that they "are aiming for 9 out of 10 of our ideas to be successful compared to 1 in 10 as a VC would." As a studio you have the ability to start seeing patterns and trends arising. When you are validating your hundredth idea, you get a sense of what does and does not make something work.

Furthermore, in the original model of entrepreneurship you have people in a garage working full-time on their ideas, but most people can not afford the luxury to do so and go without a salary for however long it takes to become revenue positive. On top of that, most of the time those ideas do not catch and you end up failing anyway. Historically there has not been true accessibility to entrepreneurship. So when you can systematically de-risk those ideas at an early stage through a start-up studio model, the opportunity to become a founder appeals to more people.

Jason shares how he has sold his first company for nine million dollars without raising any VC funding and still owning almost half of it at the moment of exit. "A VC would see that as a failure, but it is life changing. Someone has to build smaller companies too. We cannot sustain only the creation of rocket-ships and unicorns. Start-up studios go after different types of businesses, they widen the net of the capital world," he says.

* * *

Another important benefit is the reduction of overhead cost. A studio should own an infrastructure made out of pooled resources that streamline the creation process. It's in our nature as entrepreneurs to build things and see if they work. The ability to do so freely leads to a whole new level of experimentation, but that requires an infrastructure. There is and will always be a considerable overhead on doing experiments. Even the lean start-ups have costs and sometimes that could be a burden for many.

If you are trying to raise money every time you want to try something new, you might as well ask for all at once for funding for subsequent experiments. Start-up studios are naturally designed to achieve economies of scale with their support operations.

Another benefit is the pool of knowledge created. One solution found for a complex problem one of the start-ups encounters may solve several other internal issues for other start-ups housed within. Enabling the cross pollination of talent and ideas becomes significantly more important if the kind of things you are building are similar.

Once you achieve a cohesive set of capabilities that can work together such as data science, branding, legal, etc., it is much more efficient to have those people under the same roof working on multiple projects. This decreases the downtime of those employees while maintaining a consistent feeling across those companies.

A great example is Poncho, the leading conversational weather app acquired by Dirty Lemon in 2018. During its creation in Betaworks, Glitter, another project was experiencing amazing on-boarding but was facing little retention of users after the initial use. The person who designed the on-boarding strategy for Glitter ended up joining Poncho to help them with that. Under the idea of "something that works here might work there," he was able to drive growth in a project he hadn't started. Matt Hartman says that early on there is high flexibility in terms of tasks, "we work on projects related to each other. The skill overlap is present and relevant, which allows for this flexibility to happen." Matt's statement is specifically applicable to start-up studios focusing on one specific industry or vertical.

In a *Wired* article, Issie Lapowsky shares another story from Betaworks when Giphy, the popular search engine for GIFS, got so flooded with demand after launch that the whole system crashed: "It was 3 a.m. on a Saturday morning, and the Betaworks team was able to pull together an operations person from Betaworks, one of the company's hackers in residence, and an engineer from Digg, one of Betaworks' most successful portfolio companies. By the end of the weekend, not only was the system back up and running, but Giphy had four full-time staff members working on the company."[121]

121 Lapowsky, Issie. "The Next Big Thing You Missed: Tech Superstars Build 'startup Factories'". *Wired*, Nov. 25, 2014. https://www.wired.com/2014/11/startup-factories/.

Matt shared with me that the mentality during that weekend was more or less "oh, let me fix that for you real quick."

"We saved the tech infrastructure, so we could sustain the demand, and essentially printed an amazing team, all in a matter of days," shares Paul Murphy, another partner at Beta-works and CEO of Dots. "The typical process would have been, 'Let's start fundraising, and then build the team.' By that point, you've lost momentum. You can't even put into numbers how much that's worth."[122]

It is not all rosy in this world though. Knowing that it takes seven to ten years for a company to generate substantial income and or get acquired, cash flow becomes really important for a start-up studio. It's very easy to run out of money and while that doesn't really mean the studio is dead, it does force the team to take an operating role in existing projects rather than starting new ones.

The sustainability of a studio consists of being able to continuously start new projects, rather than have a one time push to create several companies and wait for a new round of capital to create a second push. In the case of Saturn V, their future as a studio is quite shaky, with resources and talent heavily tied into their portfolio. "Even though we are doing really

---

122 Ibid.

well for ourselves and our investors, we are not really doing what we were set to do," Jason shares.

The goal of a start-up studio is to replicate its ability to build successful companies. Thanks to its infrastructure and resources, start-up studios increase a start-up's chance of success and optimize its creation and growth. Start-up studios are not early stage investors, but actual co-founders. Building many companies in a row should remain the main goal of a start-up.

THE DIFFERENTIATING FACTORS

In the past two chapters we talked about how co-working spaces, incubators, and accelerators are providing value to entrepreneurial ecosystems. There are some key differences between a start-up studio and other entrepreneurial support units.

Firstly, the start-up studio does the heavy lifting in the team. From engineering and prototyping to data science and branding, the staff of the studio is acting as a hands-on co-founder. All of the components that go into validating the business opportunity, including building a team who will be able to execute, are part of the duties of the studio. By doing so, they assume accountability for the whole project, not just provide capital, some resources, and advice. In the case of a more traditional entrepreneurial support unit, it is usually up to the founder to find the talent needed to grow the business and make the most of the resources available to them.

Another important difference is the provenience of the ideas. Most of the time a start-up studio will come up with their own ideas as internal testable projects rather than having an application process where founders who are already working on something can join. Matt Hartman from Betaworks discussed with me, "People are encouraged to come work and see that is interesting to them. When you join, you'll have a specific role on a specific project, but you are free to come up with ideas or even start building something new. We are a community of builders after all. Your role could then either go with that company when it is spun out, or if you decide to stay and keep working on other projects you have that option. It's a question of passion when deciding to go or not to go full time on one of those ventures." A start-up studio is an institutional analog to a serial entrepreneur.

Thibaud Elziere, co-founder of Paris based start-up studio eFounders, talked in an online article about the difference between start-up studios and the other entrepreneurial support units. He put together a great graphic to show the interplay between those institutions on two measurements: invested capital and invested human hours.[123]

---

123 Elziere, Thibaud. "Startup Studios: The Rise of Human Capital". Medium, Apr. 22, 2015. https://medium.com/startup-studio/startup-studios-the-rise-of-human-capital-7cf71e7aee14.

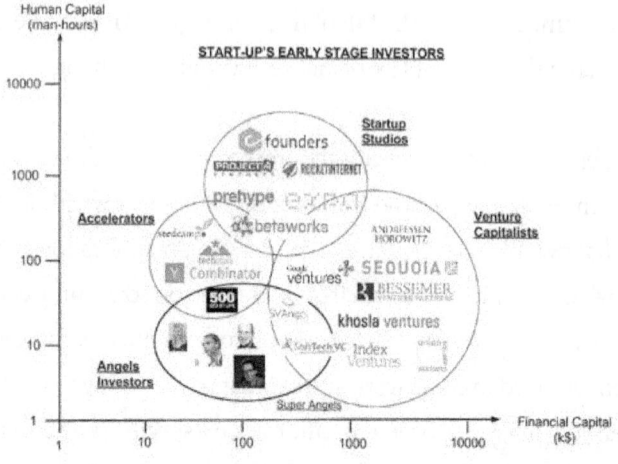

The increased focus on talent and reduced emphasis on the initial idea makes start-up studios the most suitable at following the Human Approach described earlier in this book when compared to co-working studios, incubators, and accelerators. This seems to come with financial advantages as well.

Research by start-up studio guru Attila Szigeti shows that "start-up studios can achieve higher growth score from the same amount of money. This suggests that fueling the growth of a studio company is much more cost efficient than fueling the growth of a regular start-up."[124]

---

124 Szigeti, Attila. *Start-up Studio Playbook.* 2016.

BUILDING A START-UP STUDIO

Throughout this chapter we have explored the intricacies of start-up studios, but one question remains unanswered:

What do you need to start such a thing?

As a structure, start-up studios are a very hard thing to create, with limited space for younger or more junior people. At the moment, people with the best network and enough capital best fit to start one of those units. There has to be some reputation behind the founders in order to be able to gather the necessary resources from investors, mentors, and other entrepreneurs. As rough as it may sound, you need credibility in the space to start one. It is unlikely to succeed without those connections.

People who run the studios have a tremendous level of reputation in the community with both investors and entrepreneurs. This model works when the founders who you can recruit and work with are high caliber. Ben Gilbert from PSL shares that "A+ ideas to B- CEOs will fail. The core asset of start-up studios is the ability to provide the right amount of value to some of the best entrepreneurs and start companies with them."

The talent pipeline is a core element of the studio, since it is the element that provides the unit with the people to work on those ideas. As we have seen, it is not only founders who join those units but also experts in various fields with a desire to work and help on several projects rather than just one. When analyzing the success of the famous billionaire serial entrepreneurs such as Peter Thiel, Elon Musk, Reid Hoffman, Luke Nosek, Ken Howery, and Keith Rabois the same success story emerges. "It wasn't that the PayPal mafia was uniquely different than most people, but they had a very tight, strong network that really committed to helping everyone rise," says Human Ventures founding partner and CEO Heather Hartnett. "And I think that the studio model is analogous to that."[125]

Needless to say, capital or easy access to capital is part of the foundation too. Saturn V has a network of angel investors that they can constantly tap into for different projects based on their investment profile. This brings in capital to their portfolio companies in order to encourage growth. Others are funded by wealthy entrepreneurs who decide to start building more than one company at a time.

An expert network follows close fourth because it grants the ability to expand the knowledge of the studio and its employees. Kevin, from PSL, shares that "One of the things that makes us unique is the quality and size of our network that we can tap into whenever we want."

125 Mohan, Pavithra. "Exclusive: Human Ventures elevates its woman-led startup studio with a $50 million debut fund". *Fast Company*, Feb. 28, 2019. https://www.fastcompany.com/90311721/exclusive-human-ventures-elevates-its-woman-led-startup-studio-with-a-50-million-debut-fund.

Last, but not least, a specific process of building start-ups accompanied by purposeful resources brings all the elements together and grants the studio the capacity to start developing ideas.

A studio should own an infrastructure made out of pooled resources that streamlines the creation process. Operational experience is a key factor since the success of start-ups depends on the quality and efficiency of execution on their ideas.

So what would be the checklist if you want to build a start-up studio?

- Experienced founder with a proven track record

- Talent pipeline for founders and employees

- Capital

- Network of investors and mentors

- Repeatable process of validating ideas and starting businesses

- Operational resources to streamline the previously mentioned process

It should be clear by now that start-up studios, builders, foundries, factories, or whatever you want to call them have become the new sexy thing in entrepreneurship. Understanding how they work and why they were founded in the first place became imperative for anyone working in the field. With a plethora of benefits and fewer drawbacks than typical entrepreneurial support units, start-up studios provide a new, more engaging and equitable way of helping founders build businesses.

KEY TAKEAWAYS:

- Start-up studios are not early stage investors, but actual co-founders.

- Studios are one of the hardest entrepreneurial support units to start, but also one of the most efficient with the highest rate of success.

- This model is ideal for de-risking investments in start-ups and increasing accessibility to entrepreneurship.

- The mobility of employees inside a start-up studio allows increased flexibility in the way projects are tackled.

CHAPTER 13

UNIVERSITIES

—

"If you've got an idea, start today. There's no better time than now to get going. That doesn't mean quit your job and jump into your idea 100% from day one, but there's always small progress that can be made to start the movement."

- KEVIN SYSTROM

"The art of handling university students is to make oneself appear, and this almost ostentatiously, to be treating them as adults."

- ARNOLD TOYNBEE

"I still remember that four years ago when I just entered my first year at a university in Beijing, my friend introduced me to two Chinese students studying at Harvard and the University of Virginia. I was astonished at hearing that they were starting their own company, and asked a silly question: 'How could you do this at such a young age?!' This was the first time I had met a 'student entrepreneur.'" says Jamie Wang, a graduate student at Carnegie Mellon University, in an article.[126]

As an international student from Romania, my first year in college was marked by similar questions. Coming from a country where ageism is incredibly prevalent in the business world, the concept of starting a business young was highly attractive but foreign. During my time at the University of Rochester, I ended up starting not one but two small businesses.

In the summer after my freshman year, I was on the phone with Pavel Stan, a fellow Romanian student in the U.S. and a good friend. We were chatting about the mindset that we had developed coming from a borderline-developing country to a prosperous nation like the United States. The struggles that

---

126 Wang, Jaime. "Why Entrepreneurship Is So Different between the US and China: A Comparative Cultural Perspective from a Chinese Student". *New Venturist*, Mar. 7, 2012. http://newventurist.com/2012/03/why-entrepreneurship-is-so-different-between-us-and-china-a-comparative-cultural-perspective-from-a-chinese-student/.

we faced made us resilient in the face of failure and allowed us to take advantage of many more opportunities here. This is the reason why, in both cases as we discovered during that call, other students came to us for advice.

It all started with friends, and then friends of friends, and after getting an internship at Deloitte when I was eighteen, inquiries from complete strangers started flowing in. As I could not help so many students, I had to refuse some and that's when the miracle happened:

People said they would be willing to pay for my advice.

I was shocked and called Pavel, who had an incredibly similar situation happening to him in Philadelphia, Pennsylvania at Drexel University. We decided to start a small student consulting practice named North of the Soul. After a year of being in business, Pavel left for Japan in an attempt to "find himself" and we decided to close shop until further notice.

The same summer I was on the phone with the same friend and were discussing the outrageous textbook prices in the U.S. We were comparing alternatives and systemic changes that could, at least in theory, drive the prices down. Not satisfied with anything that we found, he suggested trying to build a solution ourselves. The project was put on a short hold as we were preparing for the growth of the consulting business, but the topic came up more and more often in conversation.

Soon, we realized this was something we could be pursuing and decided to give it a try. That is how BarterOut, an ed tech start-up that builds software solutions for textbook trading and course selection, was founded. We received funding from start-up competitions, built our first product, established a network of mentors and, at our peak, employed twelve students. Almost two years later, I stepped down from the CEO position as I realized that new leadership could further the growth of the company. I was also preparing to graduate.

Even though my story is not as glamorous as the likes of Microsoft, Facebook, Yahoo, Google, Napster, or Dell, which were all founded by college students, it proves a point:

Entrepreneurship in college is possible.

The caveat is that it is hard. Even harder than "adult entrepreneurship" because the time is incredibly limited and the stress is incredibly high.

On top of that, with classes, exams, and most of the time other jobs too, starting a business takes up the evenings and nights on students' calendars. This is one of the reasons why most successful college entrepreneurs dropped out of college to pursue their start-up endeavors full time.

This is by no means encouraging people to drop out and become entrepreneurs — it is a risky bet to make — but rather acknowledges the reality of student entrepreneurship. There are success stories of people who did stay in college.

* * *

Sarah Pomeranz, co-founder of Sulis, a student start-up addressing clean water scarcity with their innovative water sterilization technology, shared that "As both a student entrepreneur and a student of entrepreneurship, I have come to understand that to fully embody entrepreneurship is to strive to leave the world better than you found it and to empower those around you to do the same. Our ability to raise $40,000 in order to fund the pilot program in Mumbai and Gujarat, India demonstrated that we possessed the grit necessary to turn this aspirational business concept into a tangible product that saves lives."[127]

In Chapter 7, I shared the story of how Alex Liberman and Austin Rief grew their college side hustle in a media start-up

---

127 "A Student Entrepreneur, And A Student Of Entrepreneurship". *Rutgers Business School*, Mar. 29, 2019. https://www.business.rutgers. edu/news/student-entrepreneur-and-student-entrepreneurship.

now boasting over one million daily readers. Asked about the challenges they faced building a company while in college, Austin also mentions the ability to go full time on their venture — "School will always be number one, and it's hard to dedicate yourself to a business when that's the case." It isn't only negatives though.

The ability to not pay themselves for two-and-a-half years granted them the opportunity and time to cheaply validate their idea and build a proof of concept. That head start was a key factor when they decided to go full time and pursue this entrepreneurial career. On top of that, their first investor was actually the University of Michigan, who provided them with initial capital and resources to get their idea off the ground.

Another great perk was the immediate connection to a pool of highly talented and driven individuals who were going through similar struggles. "I was in this program my senior year and I had the chance to meet with other student entrepreneurs. Just the ability to come together with like-minded people was incredibly beneficial," Austin recalls. When you are surrounded by people who are not actively pursuing their goals and building ventures, it's hard to stay on track and believe those things are possible.

Universities have this unique advantage of being a natural foundation for their entrepreneurial ecosystems: high intellectual capital — to be read as 'students'. One of the best things about students is that they have very big visions and want to change the world. Their challenge is to fit those crazy ideas in the time frame of a business.

The people are already there, they just need a reason and a way to come together to work on those radical ideas. We are seeing the same principle at work that Hugh Mason discovered when he moved to Singapore. The role of the universities becomes that to create the social capital, provide guidance and thus complete the equation.

SO HOW DO THEY DO THAT?

According to my research, it is a mix of resources that span from student entrepreneurship clubs, talks, and workshops to more professional units such as incubators, accelerators, and mentor networks.

Andreea Januta from Thomson Reuters Foundation reports that "Almost half of all universities now have some sort of incubator or accelerator program to support student entrepreneurs."[128] These structures are essential in order to

---

128 Januta, Andreea. "US Universities Invest In Student Entrepreneurship". *The Christian Science Monitor*, May 10, 2018. https://www.csmonitor.com/USA/Education/2018/0510/US-universities-invest-in-student-entrepreneurship.

build opportunities for young founders. They enable them to test their assumptions, fail fast, iterate, and build using human-centered design.

When looking at their entrepreneurial support programs, the most successful universities are heavily focused on delivering world-class resources and programming. It is not just the number of opportunities but the energetic implementation of those initiatives that drives students to start businesses there.

Carnegie Mellon University has a very successful incubation program called Project Olympus. It has grown from advising twenty potential start-ups a decade ago to one hundred forty in 2018. It has created more than four hundred full-time positions in the city, according to the program's director Kit Needham. All of this was possible with the buy-in of all stakeholders in the ecosystem, especially the top management of the university, which set entrepreneurship as one of their central goals.

Through my research on university entrepreneurial support units, I have found out that highly successful entrepreneurial universities do six things very well:

- They provide a space for entrepreneurship to happen, taking care of all the supporting infrastructure — from the physical location, to hardware, software, labs, financial and legal support.

- They provide lots of opportunities for students to connect with each other and with mentors — through office hours and one-on-ones with both industry experts and alumni.

- They fund many ideas and ventures by placing small bets on a lot of companies and then focusing their attention on the ones with high growth potential.

- They focus on integrating entrepreneurship in the educational component of their institutions.

- They empower students to create or work on start-ups over the summer by helping them financially.

- They support founders even after graduation and keep them in contact with the college community.

Bottom line, they are building communities. Rei Wang, former CEO of the Dorm Room Fund which s a student-focused subsidiary of First Round Capital, shared that "the money is only one of the values we provide. More important is the access to the community. DRF has the strongest community of student founders in the world. That's where our value lies." Just imagine being in the portfolio of a VC focused only on students. Having things in common with the other founders will build the foundation for great collaborations. They understand each other.

As much as we praise communities like DRF for their understanding, we need to learn how to translate that core element in universities. The people in charge of those programs and resources need to talk to the students and figure out what their needs are.

They have to listen to the students.

After all, the students are the customers of the university. As we have seen in Chapter 9, if this thing works there, it doesn't mean it will work everywhere. Universities develop unique cultures and that is evident in their entrepreneurial ecosystems. The programs that work at Stanford will not work at MIT.

We are in dire need of bespoke entrepreneurial support and until people start treating universities as ecosystems and apply the same tools they would when building start-up communities, no radical progress will be made.

EDUCATING THE STUDENT ENTREPRENEURS AND THEIR SUPPORTERS

We need to acknowledge that the student mindset might not be the best tool for building start-ups. The whole time before and during college people are asked to build on top of previous research, focusing on the scientific method as the golden rule. Most of the time, entrepreneurship is not science. The question is whether you can build something that people want to pay for. The start-up world is fundamentally different than the academic world because it is outcome driven.

We need to educate student founders and understand that they need exposure to a space that has been foreign to them most of their lives. By building cross-disciplinary groups of experts and providing mentorship resources, we can ensure they get the right amount of feedback on their execution.

So what should we teach them?

Apart from STEM education, we need to teach human design and empathy as those are the number one skills founders of any age should have. Rei Wang shares that what she wants to see in student founder is the ability to understand, motivate, and influence. Again, the human aspect of entrepreneurship is getting the attention it deserves.

Also, all the investments made are rewarding. If you think about it, DRF has the opportunity to see start-ups at the earliest stage before any other investor. The ability to find the most promising founders is enhanced for such units. There is one entity that has the chance to pick the winning stock even before the DRF, and that is the university itself.

Identifying the folks who are not afraid of going against the grain will give universities an advantage over any VC. College employees should primarily train their speed of observation. This is one of the skills that will differentiate between successful and not so successful university entrepreneurial ecosystems.

Are some universities just better positioned than others to empower entrepreneurship among their students, staff and faculty?

Absolutely!

PitchBook's 2016-2017 "Universities Report" concludes that "people rely on their most trusted connections, those whom they've known for the longest and with whom they share the deepest bonds. Such a trend could be evidenced by an increased concentration of VC-backed start-up production at the universities that are already dominators in their categories — a winner-take-all phenomenon, in other words. Those winners — in terms of entrepreneur production, of course — already benefit from geographic proximity to major sources of capital, well-regarded business schools, deeply rooted monoliths in certain industries, etcetera. Such incumbent advantages are hard to beat, which is one reason why there has been precisely no fluctuation in the ranking of the top ten university undergraduate programs between this year's installment and the last, although the actual figures have varied considerably."[129]

---

129 Universities Report 2016-2017. PitchBook. Url: https://files.pitchbook. com/pdf/PitchBook_Universities_Report_2016-2017_Edition.pdf.

DMZ, the world's best university tech start-up accelerator, is owned and operated by Ryerson University in Toronto, Canada. Since 2010, they helped grow and graduate 412 start-ups which raised $605 million in seed funding and created more than 3,750 jobs in the community. During their time at the DMZ, the start-ups acquired customers, won awards, exponentially grown their teams, and developed products and solutions that are positively changing lives and impacting businesses across Canada and abroad.

"Our work isn't fueled by a hunger for profit or recognition; it's fueled by passion. Both the DMZ staff and the start-ups work hard because we love what we do, and because we're excited about the fruits of our labor," shares Abdullah Snobar, the executive director of the program.

When asked about whether being part of a university is beneficial or not, Sherif El Tawil, DMZ's director of operations, says that "there are both opportunities and obstacles." Smaller, centralized resources such as HR, accounting, and legal are incredibly useful but as the program grows, the same resources become a drawback. They were not designed to support the exponential growth and speed of the entrepreneurial world.

Even when that is the case, universities remain a top source of entrepreneurial activity and a significant part of the attention of VCs around the world. Overall, they streamline the entrepreneurial process by making it easy and cheap for students to test their ideas and connect with others.

KEY TAKEAWAYS:

- Even though most highly successful entrepreneurial universities are close to hubs of venture capital, those who aren't can still properly support student founders.

- Universities who are making entrepreneurship a focus of the whole institution are able to not only offer more resources but more energetically implement them.

- Higher ed institutions should understand that their unique ecosystems develop unique cultures and as a result, bespoke entrepreneurial resources are needed to drive maximum value.

CONCLUSION

———

Throughout this book we have explored how entrepreneurial ecosystems around the globe are activating founders to design innovative solutions to some of the world's most pressing problems.

We broke down entrepreneurial support structures such as co-working spaces, incubators, accelerators, start-up studios, and universities in order to better understand how they can add the most value to the founders.

We followed stories of amazing innovators developing entrepreneurial communities across the globe from New Zealand, Thailand, China, and Singapore to Jamaica, Utah and Nebraska. We explored some of their cultural differences and analyzed their similarities.

We have seen how they are moving away from the traditional way of thinking about supporting founders and how they are embracing a new set of core tenants in their practice. If we were to summarize it in one word it would be "community."

The Human Approach is not rocket science. It is a return to the very basic nature of our existence and applying its teachings to the entrepreneurial industry. It is the realization that behind everything that we see in the world, there are people. All stakeholders are human and thus, breaking away from the stereotypical start-up equation, if one was even ever quantified, is the next step towards healthier entrepreneurial ecosystems around the globe.

How people live, work, and spend their money has changed dramatically over the past decade. As the line between work and non-work activities got more and more blurred, entrepreneurship as a science and art changed dramatically. The rapid expansion of the gig economy enabled new forms of entrepreneurship and made it difficult to distinguish between an entrepreneur and an independent contractor. The idea of a "founder" is being challenged to the core as we speak and entrepreneurial support resources are needed by more and more people around the world as they embark on their own creation journey.

We have come to understand that entrepreneurs are made, not born, and so are leaders. This tectonic shift in mindset is propelling us to redefine the qualifications of a founder in the 21st century.

SO WHERE ARE WE HEADED FROM HERE?

I believe it is towards an even more human approach to entrepreneurship. Technological progress will not slow down anytime soon and humans are here to stay. I predict that more and more emphasis will be put on the development of individual founders with significant attention given to their education, mental, and physical health.

I feel confident that we will see increased representation of women and historically underrepresented minorities as founders and investors and that we will move past the barrier of ageism, sexism, and racism to realize that anyone can be a creator of change. This shift we will enable more people to begin thinking of themselves as entrepreneurs in this new entrepreneurial structures — equitable, more diverse, and more accessible.

As more and more people come and live together in cities, I'm certain that we will find creative ways to bring them genuinely together, be it in co-working spaces or even co-living spaces. It will be companies like WeWork, Impact Hub, the Hive, and their likes that will be paving the way for a more connected business world. We should and will continue to run community events and bring diverse innovators together to brainstorm and build radical projects.

I believe that we will continue to tell stories and navigate the filters of social media to remain authentic. That we will continue to empower others to share theirs and build meaningful connections. That we will embrace empathy as a core tenant in interpersonal relationships with co-founders, employees, investors, mentors, suppliers and customers.

That we will take the human centered approach of designing products and services and apply it to the process of innovation itself. That we are moving towards increased customization of entrepreneurial support and a better understanding of the cultural differences of various communities and ecosystems.

That more industries will be disrupted by small, agile and innovative start-ups. That the struggles for older, established companies will not slow down anytime soon and that they will be forced to collaborate with or design their own innovation hubs.

Finally, I believe that small and medium-sized cities will have the power to develop strong entrepreneurial ecosystems. That the center of global innovation will shift East as developing countries are creating huge markets waiting for the supply to match the demand and that the local entrepreneurs will be the best equipped to address those markets.

Only time will tell us if we were right betting on a more human approach to supporting entrepreneurs. Until then, let's work towards building a better future and helping others do the same.

Remember: when they win, you win!

ACKNOWLEDGEMENTS

First and foremost, I want to thank Eric Koester for all his guidance and mentorship, and for giving me the opportunity to write this book. Serendipity brought us in the same room at the same time. That serendipity came in the form of Justin Lafazan and Dylan Gambardella, who I thank for organizing the NextGen Summit, the conference at which I met professor Koester.

Huge thanks go to the editorial team at New Degree Press! Thank you Brian Bies for bearing with me at the best and the worst of this journey and always believing this project will be completed on time. Somehow it happened. Thank you to my developmental editor, Andrew Porciaux, to my marketing editor, Ryan Porter, to my copy-editor, Abbey Murphy, and to my layout editor, Zoran Maksimovic, who all helped shape the book and saved you from reading a collection of boring stories and facts. Thank you Lyn Solares, Leila Summers, and ChandaElaine Spurlock for all of the behind-the-scenes work you put in to get this project finalized.

A big round of applause goes to the incredibly talented cover designer Srdjan Filipovic for adding color to the exterior of my work and to the amazing photographer Jiangyong Xu (aka Wayne) for the author headshots.

Thank you to all the amazing innovators that took time in their busy schedules to speak with me and share their expertise: Abdullah Snobar, Austin Rief, Ben Elowitz, Ben Gilbert, Cyril Ebersweiler, Dan Khan, Desiree Frieson, Doug Chambers, Haley Hoffman Smith, Howard Love, Hugh Mason, Iulia Tudor, Jama Mohamed, Jason Ford, Jeff Slobotski, Jess Williamson, John Schloff, Jonathan Maxim, Julia Maddox, Julian Clayton, Keith Berry, Keith Corso, Kevin Leneway, Kyle Herron, Leanne Robers, Mark Lazar, Mark Wilson, Matthew Hartman, Mike Lightman, Mike Riedlinger, Noel Joyce, Rachel Jaffe, Rei Wang, Ryan Kushner, Sherif El Tawil, Sunny Su, and Vince Scafaria.

Thank you to the early readers who provided critical feedback on this book: Elizabeth Meyer, Cristian Mandachescu, Julia Maddox, and Alexandra Prundaru. This book was a team effort!

Thank you to my family, especially my mother Cristina and my father Bogdan for all the support given throughout my life. Nothing would be possible without you. Thank you to Nadia, Cami, Noru, Ada, Andu, Deni, Catalin, Eric and Delia for always being there for me. Magda, Cristi, and Ion, I know you are smiling watching me grow up from above — this is for you too, I miss you!

A huge thank you to my mentors: Mike Lightman, Cristian Mandachescu, Elizabeth Meyer, Julia Maddox, and Grace Nicholson. I deeply cherish your guidance!

Thank you to the most amazing friends one can hope to have, for their moral support and all their encouragements: Arif Kodza, Ali Biashad, Michael Gilbert, Nate Barnes, Giovanni Ilaqua, Annie Hamburgen, Sam Hirschhorn, Beatriz Gil Gonzalez, Kamel Awayda, Olavi Hangula, Bogdan Miron, Mihai Leorda, Cristina Pogorevici, Pavel Stan, Maria Muller, Genessis Galindo, Juan Pueyo, Rachel Goodman, Lara Andree, Amro Bayoumy, Mike Chung, Sophia McRae, Marc Haddad, Mira Amin, Sarmishtha Rukimani Prathivadhi Bhayankaram Venkatesh, Shurik Zavriyev, Gerardo Zambrano, Darren Huang, Muhammad Hadi, Nick Frankiewicz, Nate Leopold, Clara Gil Gonzalez, Nic Hesse, Ivona Mihaescu, John Cole and Genesis Peguero.

Thank you to my amazing brothers in Beta Theta Pi for always being there for me. I was an only child before I came to the University of Rochester and found you! Forever yours in _kai_ proud to be a Beta!

Thank you Daniela Bordei for helping me get to the United States and thus gain access to all these amazing opportunities. I will always owe you big time!

Thank you to the amazing teachers and professors who shared their knowledge with me: Daniela Moraru, Petre Simion, Ron Schmidt, Dr. Christopher Niemiec, Heidi Tribunella, Dr. Michael Rizzo, Dr. Kate Phillips, John Schloff, Dr. Jaewoo Kim, Dr. Roy Jones, and Dr. James Prinzi.

Thank you to my amazing co-workers at iZone for handling all my breakdowns as I missed some deadlines for this book: Anush Mehrabyan, Deniz Cegniz, Ellen Liao, Mike Arinarkin, Maria Hackett, Dewey Bazirake, Shannon Lue Chee Lip, Maggie Peng, Michael Keane, Ewin Joseph, Allie Fredrickson, Victoria Ter-Ovanesyan, and Zoe Tzetzis. Thank you Grant Dever for being an amazing manager, fellow author, and co-founder of the Rochester Creators project. Thank you Dean Mavrinac for believing in this project since day one and for all the support you offered.

Thank you to the team at BarterOut for offering me an amazing learning opportunity as we discovered how to be entrepreneurs together: Pavel Stan, Annie Hamburgen, Luis Nova,

Duncan Grubbs, Daniel Munoz, Nikolai Draganov, Melissa Kagaju, Zixu Chen, Zino Hu, Shagun Bose, May Shin Lyan, Aman Shrestha and Zacqueline Baldwin-Sease.

Thank you to all the staff at the University of Rochester who made this journey so amazing: Hillary Tatar, Laura Ballou, Heather Maclin, Brian Magee, Anne-Marie Algier, Stacey Fisher, Joe Testani, David Cota-Buckout, John DiSarro, Rose Piacente, Juliane Schnibbe, Meghan Plate, Kathy Driscoll, Heidi Mergenthaler, Matthew Spielmann, Vice Provost Moore, Dean Runner, and Dean Burns.

This book wouldn't have been made possible without the amazing people who believed in this project and pre-ordered this book before it was even finished and sent to print. Your financial support made this book and it's publication possible. Those amazing campaign sponsors are listed below:

BRONZE SPONSORS

Arif Kodza	Paul Stelian Tanu
Emily Ann Kumpf	Lia Hancianu
John Schloff	Ana Guilandeaux
Jimmy Yang	Andrei Stanescu
Elianor Aoun	Yi Gu

SILVER SPONSORS

Sam Hirschhorn	Rachel Jaffe
Eric Koester	Giovanni Ilacqua
Kate McCarthy	Patrick Ostie
Dan LaSalle	Diana Deoki
Maria Muller	Mary Ann Mavrinac
Grant Dever	Ali Biashad
Dax Emerson	Cristi Dragan
Iulia Dobrescu	Isabella Andrino
Ian Brodka	Anush Mehrabyan
Michael Chung	Michael Gilbert
Annmarie Hamburgen	Bogdan Miron

I'd like to especially thank the people who invested more in my publishing and pre-ordered multiple copies of my book. With special thanks to the:

GOLD SPONSORS

Jane & Joel Hirschhorn	Alina Oprina
Bogdan & Cristina Cazacu	Scott Saucier

Thank you to everyone. Your financial support allowed me to transform countless pages of notes and interviews into the book you are about to read.

NOTES

———

INTRODUCTION

1. Garing, Caleb. "Airbnb Founder: Company "Wasn't Supposed to Be the Big Idea."" *Vanity Fair*, Oct. 2014. https://www.vanityfair.com/news/tech/2014/10/airbnb-founder-big-idea-logo.

2. Global Accelerator Report 2016. *Gust*. Url: http://gust.com/accelerator_reports/2016/global/.

3. Global Report 2017/18. *Global Entrepreneurship Monitor*. Url: https://www.gemconsortium.org/report

4. Hathaway, Ian. "What Start-up Accelerators Really Do." *Harvard Business Review*, Mar. 01, 2016. https://hbr.org/2016/03/what-start-up-accelerators-really-do.

5. Loten, Angus. "Search for Doctor Leads to Yelp." *The Wall Street Journal*, Nov. 14, 2012. https://www.wsj.com/articles/SB10001424127887324595904578117512589717352.

6. Szigeti, Attila. *Start-up Studio Playbook*. 2016.

CHAPTER 1: WHY INNOVATE?

1. Brown, Tim. "*Change by Design: How Design Thinking Transforms Organizations and Inspires Innovation*". HarperBusiness, 2009.

2. Richmond, Shane. "Jonathan Ive Interview: Simplicity Isn't Simple". *The Telegraph*, May 23, 2012. https://www.telegraph.co.uk/technology/apple/9283706/Jonathan-Ive-interview-simplicity-isnt-simple.html.

3. Thompson, Derek. "Google X and The Science of Radical Creativity". *The Atlantic*, Nov. 2017. https://www.theatlantic.com/magazine/archive/2017/11/x-google-moonshot-factory/540648/.

4. US Census Bureau. Start-up Firms Created Over 2 Million Jobs in 2015. Sep. 20, 2017. Url: https://www.census.gov/newsroom/press-releases/2017/business-dynamics.html.

CHAPTER 2: A VERY BRIEF WALK THROUGH HISTORY

1. Becerra, Jorge. "The Digital Revolution Is Not About Technology – It's About People". *World Economic Forum*, Mar. 28, 2017. https://www.weforum.org/agenda/2017/03/the-digital-revolution-is-not-about-technology-it-s-about-people/.

2. Graham, Paul. "The Future of Start-up Funding". *Essays of Paul Graham*, Aug. 2010. http://www.paulgraham.com/future.html.

3. Graham, Paul. "Why There Aren't More Googles". *Essays of Paul Graham*, Apr. 2008. http://www.paulgraham.com/googles.html.

4. Harnett, Heather. "The Rise of "The Platform" for Venture Capital Funds". *Forbes*, Sep. 28, 2017. https://www.forbes.com/sites/heatherhartnett/2017/09/28/the-rise-of-the-platform-for-venture-capital-funds/#1def6edb4484.

5. Katz, Lawrence and Alan Krueger. "The Rise and Nature of Alternative Work Arrangements in the United States, 1995-2015," *NBER* Working Paper No. 22667, September 2016.

6. Morning Brew newsletter on May 10, 2019. Url: https://www.morningbrew.com/latest/archive/2019/05/10/bump/.

7. Price, Robert. "What Is The History of Entrepreneurship in America?". *Global Entrepreneurship Institute*, Nov. 9, 2015. https://news.gcase. org/2015/11/09/what-is-the-history-of-entrepreneurship-in-america/.

8. Radler Cohen, Judy. "A Brief History of Venture Capital." *Financial Poise*, Nov. 21, 2018. https://www.financialpoise. com/a-brief-history-of-venture-capital/.

9. The United States of Entrepreneurs Special Report 2009. *The Economist*. Url: https://www.economist.com/special-report/2009/03/14/ the-united-states-of-entrepreneurs.

CHAPTER 3: STRUGGLES TO INNOVATE

1. Bachega, Hugo. "The Last Blockbuster: 'I'm Proud That We've Survived'." *BBC News*, Aug. 16, 2018. https://www.bbc.com/news/ world-us-canada-45175194.

2. Bennett, Frazer, Anita Chandraker, Andy Katz and Hsiu Mei Wong. "Innovation Matters." *PA Consulting*, 2016. https://www.paconsulting.com/ insights/2016/innovation-matters/.

3. Deeb, George. "The 5 Reasons Big Companies Struggle With Innovation." *Forbes*, Jan. 8, 2014. https://www.forbes.com/sites/ georgedeeb/2014/01/08/the-five-reasons-big-companies-strug-gle-with-innovation/#31d697702958.

4. Lucero, Diego. "Why Blockbuster Failed." *Siam Tek*. https://www.siamtek. com/why-blockbuster-failed/.

5. Schorn, Daniel. "The Brain Behind Netflix." *CBS News*, Dec. 01, 2006. https://www.cbsnews.com/news/the-brain-behind-netflix/.

6. Vozza, Stephanie . "The Random Events That Sparked 8 of the World's Biggest Start-ups." *Fast Company*, Nov. 03, 2014. https://www.fastcompany.com/3037896/ the-random-events-that-sparked-8-of-the-worlds-biggest-start-ups.

CHAPTER 4: DIVERSITY & INCLUSION

1. Brown, Tim. *Change by Design: How Design Thinking Transforms Organizations and Inspires Innovation.* HarperBusiness, 2009.

2. DuBow, Wendy and Allison-Scott Pruitt. "The Comprehensive Case for Investing More VC Money in Women-Led Startups". *Harvard Business Review*, Sep. 18, 2017. https://hbr.org/2017/09/the-comprehensive-case-for-investing-more-vc-money-in-women-led-startups.

3. JPMorgan Chase & Co. and ICIC Report. "Creating Inclusive High-Tech Incubators and Accelerators: Strategies to Increase Participation Rates Women and Minority Entrepreneurs". 2016.

4. Kushner, Ryan. *Accelerate This!: A Super Not Boring Guide To Startup Accelerators And Clean Energy Entrepreneurship.* CreateSpace Independent Publishing Platform, 2018.

5. Nathan, Max and Neil Lee. "*Cultural Diversity, Innovation, And Entrepreneurship: Firm-level Evidence From London*". Economic Geography 89, no. 4 (2013): 367-394.

6. Østergaard, Christian, Bram Timmermans and Kari Kristinsson. "*Does a different view create something new? The effect of employee diversity on innovation*". Research Policy 40, no. 3 (2011): 500-509.

7. Quintana-García, Cristina and Carlos Benavides-Velasco. "*Innovative Competence, Exploration and Exploitation: The Influence of Technological Diversification*". Research Policy 37, (2008): 492-507.

8. Ramasamy, Bala and Matthew Yeung. "*Diversity and Innovation*". Applied Economics Letters 23, no. 14 (2016): 1037–1041.

CHAPTER 5: NETWORKS, MENTORS & PARTNERS

1. Eesley, Charles and Yanbo Wang. "*Social Influence In Career Choice: Evidence From A Randomized Field Experiment On Entrepreneurial Mentorship*". Research Policy 46, no. 3 (2017): 636-650.

2. Harnett, Heather. "The Rise of "The Platform" for Venture Capital Funds". *Forbes*, Sep. 28, 2017. https://www.forbes.com/sites/heatherhartnett/2017/09/28/the-rise-of-the-platform-for-venture-capital-funds/#1def6edb4484.

3.   Manning, Stephanie. "Why VC Firms Are Invest-
      ing In Platform To Compete". *Forbes*, May 8, 2019.
      https://www.forbes.com/sites/valleyvoices/2019/05/08/
      why-vc-firms-are-investing-in-platform/#507300342b94.

4.   Ting, Song Xiao, Liu Feng, and Wang Qin. "*The Effect of Entrepreneur
      Mentoring and its Determinants in the Chinese Context*". Management
      Decision 55, no. 7 (2017): 1410-1425.

CHAPTER 6: EMPATHY, CULTURE & SUCCESS

1.   Beccera, Jorge. "The Digital Revolution Is Not About Tech-
      nology – It's About People". *World Economic Forum*,
      Mar. 28, 2017. https://www.weforum.org/agenda/2017/03/
      the-digital-revolution-is-not-about-technology-it-s-about-people/.

2.   Boehm, Julia and Sonja Lyubomirsky. "*Does Happiness Promote Career
      Success?*". Journal of Career Assessment 16, no. 1 (2008): 101-116.

3.   Borman, Walter, Loiuse Penner, Tammy Allen and Stephan Motowidlo.
      "*Personality Predictors Of Citizenship Performance*". International Journal
      of Selection and Assessment 9, no. 1-2 (2001): 52-69.

4.   Chatman, Jennifer and Sandra Eunyoung Cha. "*Leading by Leveraging
      Culture*". California Management Review 45, no. 4 (2003): 20–34.

5.   Cravens, Karen, Elizabeth Goad Oliver, Shigehiro Oishi and Jeanine Stew-
      art. "*Workplace Culture Mediates Performance Appraisal Effectiveness and
      Employee Outcomes: A Study in a Retail Setting*". Journal of Management
      Accounting Research 27, no. 2 (2015): 1–34.

6.   Ganster, Daniel and Christopher Rosen. "*Work Stress and Employee
      Health: A Multidisciplinary Review*". Journal of Management 39, no. 5
      (2013): 1085-1122.

7.   Gibson, James, John Ivancevich, James Donnelly and Robert Konopaske.
      "*Organizations: Behavior, Structure, Processes*". McGraw-Hill, 2012.

8.   Glazer, Emily and Christina Rexrode. "As Regulators Focus on Culture,
      Wall Street Struggles to Define It". *Wall Street Journal*, Feb. 1, 2015. https://
      www.wsj.com/articles/as-regulators-focus-on-culture-wall-street-strug-
      gles-to-define-it-1422838659.

9.   Graen, George and Miriam Grace. *"Positive Industrial and Organizational Psychology: Designing for Tech-Savvy, Optimistic, and Purposeful Millennial Professionals' Company Cultures".* Industrial and Organizational Psychology 8, no. 3 (2015): 395-408.

10. Jensen, Michael and William Meckling. *"Theory of the Firm: Managerial Behavior, Agency Costs and Ownership Structure".* Journal of Financial Economics 3, no. 4 (1976): 305-360.

11. Scott, Diane. *"The Managers Role In Increasing Happiness In The Workplace".* Stat Bulletin 78, no. 12 (2009): 11-13.

12. Strigl, Dennis. *"Results Drive Happiness: Managers Who Focus On Getting Results From Their Team Will Have Happy Employees".* HR Magazine 56, no. 10 (2011): 113.

13. Townley, Wendy. "Big Omaha: Bringing Together Designers, Tech Giants, Startups, and Investors". *Omaha Magazine,* May 24, 2017. https://omahamagazine.com/articles/big-omaha/.

14. Winkler, Rolfe. "Zenefits Once Told Employees: No Sex in Stairwells". *Wall Street Journal,* Feb. 22, 2016. https://www.wsj.com/articles/zenefits-once-told-employees-no-sex-in-stairwells-1456183097.

CHAPTER 7: DRIVE, MINDSET & MENTAL HEALTH

1.   Abel, Ted, Robbert Havekes, Jared Saletin and Matthew Walker, *"Sleep, Plasticity and Memory from Molecules to Whole-Brain Networks".* Current Biology 23, no. 17 (2013): R774-R788.

2.   Arayama, Yuko and Panos Mourdoukoutas. *"China Against Herself: Innovation or Imitation in Global Business?".* Praeger, 1999.

3.   Cabanas, Edgar and José-Carlos Sánchez-González. *"Inverting The Pyramid Of Needs: Positive Psychology's New Order For Labor Success".* Psicothema 28, no. 2 (2016): 107.

4.   Chapman, Jake. "Investors And Entrepreneurs Need To Address The Mental Health Crisis In Startup Culture". *Techcrunch,* Jan. 2019. https://techcrunch.com/2018/12/30/investors-and-entrepreneurs-need-to-address-the-mental-health-crisis-in-startup-culture/.

5. Freeman, Michael, Sheri Johnson, Paige Staudenmaier and Mackenzie Zisser. *"Are Entrepreneurs "Touched with Fire"?"*. Pre-publication manuscript, 2015.

6. Frey, Erin. "The Investor Pledge for Mental Health". *Medium*, May 30, 2017. https://medium.com/kip-blog/ the-investor-pledge-for-mental-health-a59edef02076.

7. Grant, Heidi. "How to Make Yourself Work When You Just Don't Want To". *Harvard Business Review*, Feb. 14, 2014. https://hbr.org/2014/02/ how-to-make-yourself-work-when-you-just-dont-want-to.

8. Kasser, Tim and Richard Ryan. *"Further Examining the American Dream: Differential Correlates of Intrinsic and Extrinsic Goals"*. Personality and Social Psychology Bulletin 22, (1996): 280-287.

9. Kováč, Ladislav. *"The Biology Of Happiness: Chasing Pleasure And Human Destiny"*. European Molecular Biology Organization 13, no. 4 (2012): 297-301.

10. Krause, Adam, Eti Ben Simon, Bryce Mander, Stephanie Greer, Jared Saletin, Andrea Goldstein-Piekarski and Matthew Walker. *"The Sleep-deprived Human Brain"*. Nature Reviews Neuroscience 18, no. 7 (2017): 404+.

11. Lee, Yong Suk and Chuck Eesley. *"The Persistence Of Entrepreneurship And Innovative Immigrants"*. Research Policy 47, no. 6 (2018): 1032-1044.

12. Niemiec, Christopher, Richard Ryan and Edward Deci. *"The Path Taken: Consequences of Attaining Intrinsic and Extrinsic Aspirations in Post-college Life"*. Journal of Research in Personality 43, (2009): 291-306.

13. Snobar, Abdullah. "Getting Honest About Mental Health In The World Of Tech Startups". *Forbes*, Aug. 8, 2018. https://www.forbes.com/sites/ forbestechcouncil/2018/08/08/getting-honest-about-mental-health-in-the-world-of-tech-startups/#65c919036641a.

14. Tank, Aytekin. "What I Learned About Procrastination While Scaling My Startup To 4.2 Million Users". *Medium*, Nov. 5, 2018. https://medium.com/ swlh/what-i-learned-about-procrastination-while-scaling-my-startup-to-4-2-million-users-b07ba29309e.

15. Thiel, Peter and Blake Masters. *"Zero to One: Notes on Startups, or How to Build the Future"*. Currency, 2014.

16. Wang, Serenitie and Daniel Shane. "Jack Ma Endorses China's Controversial 12 Hours A Day, 6 Days A Week Work Culture". *CNN*, Apr. 15, 2019. https://www.cnn.com/2019/04/15/business/jack-ma-996-china/index.html.

17. Wang, Xiao. "U.S. and China Startup Scenes: The Difference". *The Asian Entrepreneur*, Apr. 20, 2016. https://www.asianentrepreneur.org/differences-u-s-china-startup-scenes/.

CHAPTER 8: ASSUMPTIONS, ITERATIONS & PIVOTS

1. Graham, Paul. "How to Be an Expert in a Changing World". *Essays of Paul Graham*, Dec. 2014. http://www.paulgraham.com/ecw.html.

2. Richmond, Shane. "Jonathan Ive Interview: Simplicity Isn't Simple". *The Telegraph*, May 23, 2012. https://www.telegraph.co.uk/technology/apple/9283706/Jonathan-Ive-interview-simplicity-isnt-simple.html.

CHAPTER 9: DEVELOPING

ENTREPRENEURIAL COMMUNITIES

1. Chabot, Steve. "The Rise of Entrepreneurial Communities". *Techcrunch*, 2015. https://techcrunch.com/2015/10/03/the-rise-of-entrepreneurial-communities/.

2. Dowling, Savannah. "Utah's Tech Legacy Is Bringing Exits, Funding, And Startups". *Crunchbase News*, May 23, 2019. https://news.crunchbase.com/news/utahs-tech-legacy-is-bringing-exits-funding-and-startups/.

3. Drexler, Alejandro, Greg Fischer, and Antoinette Schoar. "*Keeping It Simple: Financial Literacy and Rules of Thumb*". American Economic Journal: Applied Economics 6, no. 2 (2014): 1-31.

4. From Jeff's personal website. https://www.jeffslobotski.com/.

5. Jing, Meng and Amanda Lee. "Where is China's Silicon Valley?". *South China Morning Post*, Aug. 12, 2017. https://www.scmp.com/tech/start-ups/article/2106494/where-chinas-silicon-valley.

6. Slobotski, Jeff. "First There Was Silicon Valley. Then Silicon Alley. Now… the Case for Building Silicon Prairie". *Time Magazine*, Jun. 19, 2012. http://business.time.com/2012/06/19/first-there-was-silicon-valley-then-silicon-alley-now-the-case-for-building-silicon-prairie/.

CHAPTER 10: CO-WORKING SPACES

1. 2019 Global Impact Report. WeWork. Url: https://www.wework.com/newsroom/posts/2019-global-impact-report.

2. 68% of the world population projected to live in urban areas by 2050. United Nations Department of Economic and Social Affairs. Url: https://www.un.org/development/desa/en/news/population/2018-revision-of-world-urbanization-prospects.html.

3. Bacevice, Peter, Gretchen Spreitzer, Hilary Hendricks and Daniel Davis. "How Coworking Spaces Affect Employees' Professional Identities". *Harvard Business Review*, Apr. 17, 2019. https://hbr.org/2019/04/how-coworking-spaces-affect-employees-professional-identities.

4. Biophilic Design in the Workplace. Human Spaces. Url: http://www.usailighting.com/stuff/contentmgr/files/1/c3f5c565a2f50b69c44dd5d3a12c6fe9/misc/biophilicdesign_humanspaces.pdf.

5. Brown, Tim. Change by Design: How Design Thinking Transforms Organizations and Inspires Innovation. *HarperBusiness*, 2009.

6. Campbell, Lindsay and Anne Wiesen. "*Restorative Commons: Creating Health And Well-being Through Urban Landscapes*". Gen. Tech. Rep. NRS-P-39 U.S. Department of Agriculture, (2011): 278.

7. Number of coworking spaces worldwide from 2005 to 2020. *Statista*. Url: https://www.statista.com/statistics/554273/number-of-coworking-spaces-worldwide/.

8. Meeting Expectations – What Employees Really Expect From Their Workplace. *K2 Space*. Url: https://k2space.co.uk/knowledge/meeting-expectations/.

9. Morris, Keiko and Eliot Brown. "WeWork Surpasses JPMorgan as Biggest Occupier of Manhattan Office Space". *Wall Street Journal*, Sep. 18, 2018. https://www.wsj.com/articles/wework-surpasses-jpmorgan-as-biggest-occupier-of-manhattan-office-space-1537268401.

10. Wilson, Edward. *Biophilia: The Human Bond With Other Species*. Harvard University Press, 1984.

CHAPTER 11: INCUBATORS & ACCELERATORS

1. Cohen, Susan. "*What Do Accelerators Do? Insights from Incubators and Angels*". Innovations: Technology, Governance, Globalization 8, no. 3 (2013): 19-25.

2. Global Accelerator Report 2016. *Gust*. Url: http://gust.com/accelerator_reports/2016/global/.

3. Gonzalez-Uribe, Juanita and Michael Leatherbee. "*The Effects of Business Accelerators on Venture Performance: Evidence from Start-Up Chile*". The Review of Financial Studies 31, no. 4 (2018): 1566–1603.

4. Hathaway, Ian. "What Startup Accelerators Really Do". *Harvard Business Review*, Mar. 01, 2016. https://hbr.org/2016/03/what-startup-accelerators-really-do.

5. Kushner, Ryan. *Accelerate This!: A Super Not Boring Guide To Startup Accelerators And Clean Energy Entrepreneurship*. CreateSpace Independent Publishing Platform, 2018.

6. Livingston, Jessica. "Congrats Dropbox!". *Y Combinator Blog*, Mar. 23, 2018. https://blog.ycombinator.com/congratsdropbox/.

7. Tom, Mikey. "One-third of U.S. startups that raised a Series A in 2015 went through an accelerator". *PitchBook*, Feb. 5, 2016. https://pitchbook.com/news/articles/one-third-of-us-startups-that-raised-a-series-a-in-2015-went-through-an-accelerator.

8. Wright, Mike and Israel Dori. *Accelerators: Successful Venture Creation and Growth*. Edward Elgar Pub, 2018.

CHAPTER 12: START-UP STUDIOS

1. Crook, Jordan. "FKTRY Wants To Be A New Type Of Startup Studio". *Techcrunch*, 2018. https://techcrunch.com/2018/05/17/fctry-wants-to-be-a-new-type-of-startup-studio/.

2. Elziere, Thibaud. "Startup Studios: The Rise of Human Capital". *Medium*, Apr. 22, 2015. https://medium.com/startup-studio/startup-studios-the-rise-of-human-capital-7cf71e7aee14.

3. Lapowsky, Issie. "The Next Big Thing You Missed: Tech Superstars Build 'startup Factories'". *Wired*, Nov. 25, 2014. https://www.wired.com/2014/11/startup-factories/.

4. Mohan, Pavithra. "Exclusive: Human Ventures elevates its woman-led startup studio with a $50 million debut fund". *Fast Company*, Feb. 28, 2019. https://www.fastcompany.com/90311721/exclusive-human-ventures-elevates-its-woman-led-startup-studio-with-a-50-million-debut-fund.

5. Startup Studio 2.0: An Industry Overview And Analysis Of The Next Phase Of Developing Startup Studios. *KML Research*, 2015.

6. Szigeti, Attila. *Start-up Studio Playbook*. 2016.

7. "The Man in The Arena" at the Theodore Roosevelt Center at Dickinson State University. Url: https://www.theodorerooseveltcenter.org/Learn-About-TR/TR-Encyclopedia/Culture-and-Society/Man-in-the-Arena.aspx.

CHAPTER 13: UNIVERSITIES

1. "A Student Entrepreneur, And A Student Of Entrepreneurship". Rutgers Business School, Mar. 29, 2019. https://www.business.rutgers.edu/news/student-entrepreneur-and-student-entrepreneurship.

2. Januta, Andreea. "US Universities Invest In Student Entrepreneurship". The Christian Science Monitor, May 10, 2018. https://www.csmonitor.com/USA/Education/2018/0510/US-universities-invest-in-student-entrepreneurship.

3. Universities Report 2016-2017. PitchBook. Url: https://files.pitchbook.com/pdf/PitchBook_Universities_Report_2016-2017_Edition.pdf.

4. Wang, Jaime. "Why Entrepreneurship Is So Different between the US and China: A Comparative Cultural Perspective from a Chinese Student". New Venturist, Mar. 7, 2012. http://newventurist.com/2012/03/why-entrepreneurship-is-so-different-between-us-and-china-a-comparative-cultural-perspective-from-a-chinese-student/.

www.ingramcontent.com/pod-product-compliance
Lightning Source LLC
Chambersburg PA
CBHW071520180526
45171CB00002B/324